No Map Just Vision

Verses Kindler Publication

Verses Kindler Publication

Website: www.verseskindlerpublication.com

No Map Just Vision

By: Capt. Pradeep Singh

ISBN: 978-93-49532-64-9

1st Edition

Price: INR 299/$15

DISCLAIMER

No Map Just Vision is authored by Capt. Pradeep Singh. The entirety of this published work comprises the original content of the author, who has undertaken diligent efforts in its editing. The characters depicted herein may be fictitious or inspired by real events; however, they are not intended to cause offense or represent any prejudice against any caste or system. Any similarity to the names of actual individuals, locations, or institutions is purely coincidental and serves the narrative. The author bears sole responsibility for the originality of this work; the publisher assumes no liability thereof.

Table of Contents

Chapter 1: The First Sparks of Ambition and Resistance

Sometimes greatness doesn't begin with poverty; it begins with comparison.

I wasn't lacking food or shelter. I was lacking peace. Every moment of watching someone else succeed sparked something inside me. A quiet discomfort that would eventually become ambition. That discomfort didn't scream. It whispered. And then it grew loud enough to drown everything else.

I wasn't born poor. That's a statement people don't normally expect to hear at the beginning of a success story. But my path wasn't one of poverty; it was a path of comparison. My grandfather was a man of honor. People might even say that he was feared, but in such a manner that he had dignity. He operated businesses, took care of his things well, and held his head high. Our extended family depended on him. But my father, by principle, by pride, by something I have now realized as silent revolt, never accepted a rupee from him. Not one. And that changed everything.

We weren't in want. But we weren't soaring either. Life wasn't desperate or lavish. It was comfortable, but strained. We shared a joint family with cousins who somehow had everything a shade better. A slightly larger scooter. A slightly newer refrigerator. A slightly trendier school bag. It wasn't said, but you could feel it, always, this relentless air of comparison. It permeates your skin without you realizing it. It becomes intimate. When you are a child, even the tiniest differences feel significant.

We were in metro cities during my earliest years, cities that moved quickly, introduced you to dreams you didn't know about yet, and had a subtext of ambition in their streets. But when my dad got shifted, we shifted to a Tier 2 city. It was no glamour. It didn't glow. It had depth, though, our depth. Our family was famous there. Our name meant something. And our kin? They were all around. With familiarity, there was proximity. And with proximity, comparison. Constant, casual, endless.

It was in that setting, veiled in tradition and family norms, that I began to distance myself from what was deemed 'normal.' Something within me started to resist, not loudly at first, but acutely. I wasn't rebelling for the sake of theatrics. I was just starting to notice the script and to realize I didn't want to obey it. I didn't want to be instructed where my place was. I didn't want my life compared to a cousin's moped or a neighbor's government career. I wanted my own standard.

I began to engage in street altercations. Not that I was aggressive, but because I couldn't tolerate being instructed to retreat. I asked awkward questions at school. I questioned authority. I hung around like a typical backbencher but surprised everybody by topping the list. That paradox became my signature. Teachers didn't know if they should suspend me or give me a prize. I was bruised on the knuckles and had certificates stuffed in my pockets. I was feared and admired. I wasn't uncouth. I knew.

That's what defined me. And that's what freed me.

I became a person who asked questions, who looked beyond procedure, who noticed that there wasn't one kind of person meant to be successful. I noticed people around me accept boundaries. I did not. My appetite did not come from poverty, but from close proximity to privilege. Seeing relatives become successful, live in nicer homes, dine at nicer restaurants, I did not feel envy. I felt something else. A flame. A question. If they could, why not I?

It wasn't arrogance. It was a purpose. Quiet, burning, and impossible to ignore.

The one person who managed to keep me anchored through all this was my mother. She had a way of handling my restlessness that didn't involve suppression. She didn't tell me to stop dreaming. She didn't tell me to behave. She told me to rise, but with grace. She was the one who taught me that in order to defeat someone, you don't necessarily have to delete their success, but produce something more. "Don't erase someone else's line," she said. "Draw a bigger one." These words resonated with me more than anything I read in any textbook.

Her presence defined my compass. She didn't try to dictate my ambition, and instead taught me to guide it. She employed humor as tact. "The best thing about wealthy relatives," she'd smile and chuckle, "is they won't borrow money from you. And the better part? You'll always have somebody to discuss." That mindset, it didn't simply brighten the mood; it provided me with a different perspective. A model for viewing the world in which comparison might be possible and also compassion, where ambition needn't be paid for with dignity.

In so many ways, my mother provided me with the emotional ammunition to endure an environment that did not encourage outliers. She granted me permission to be ambitious in a society that got ambition confused with rebellion. And most importantly, she taught me to respect myself when others could not relate to me. She knew that being amongst wealth was not a curse; it was a mirror. And I could get lost in it or learn from it.

As I got older, I started to understand the intangible walls that cut me off weren't strictly economic; they were cultural. Predictability was the religion of our world. You were meant to complete school, get a good job, get married at the right time, acquire some gold, and lead a stable life. Stability was the ultimate goal. Risk was feared. Dreaming too much wasn't just frowned upon; it was viewed as dangerous. There was a script, and you had to follow it.

But I couldn't. Whenever I attempted to conform, something within me rebelled. I didn't want to stand out. I just wanted to breathe. To live a life that was mine, not one dictated to me by somebody else's fears. My insurrection wasn't against my family. It was against complacency. Against fear. Against settling too quickly for too little.

What I possessed was faith. But I did not possess resources. That chasm between what I was convinced I could accomplish and what I really had was enormous. And it stung. I knew I could fly. I just wasn't sure how to construct the wings. There was no guidebook. No guru. No safety net. But there was faith. And for me, that was enough.

That gap did not close soon. It took years of self-directed development, errors, and brutal lessons. But ultimately, I came to see that the very absence of privilege had become my advantage. While others were cruising on their networks, I was honing myself on hunger. I had to work harder. I had to learn quicker. I had to trust my instinct because no one was providing me with playbooks.

One specific event, however minor in the large story of life, was a turning point. I had taken a scooter booking in my teens. Demand was then extremely high, and waiting times ran into months. I did not urgently need it; I had just recently obtained a booking. Then, one afternoon, someone approached me. He asked me for ten times the booking price in cash if I sold it to him.

I sold it right away.

It wasn't the money that thrilled me. It was the epiphany. That scarcity gives value. That timing is everything. That by simply noticing, you can notice what others don't. That deal wasn't giant in terms of numbers. But it was gigantic in what I learned. Business, I understood, wasn't about possessing something. It was about noticing something. Noticing it before everybody else did. Doing in others' uncertainty. That instant provided my first experience of control. Of demand reading. Of value understanding. That one scooter sale sowed a seed that would quietly germinate in the background for years to come.

That scooter moment did not make me feel successful. It made me feel alert. It taught me that I did not need to wait for a job or title to generate value. That I didn't require permission to make decisions. It was not merely a transaction, but a transformation. For the first time, I was a player and not merely a spectator in the game of life. That freedom, that notion of agency, of controlling a moment, of perceiving something that other people didn't, it was habit-forming. Unknowingly, in silence, the concept of entrepreneurship started making itself at home in my bones.

But at that time, it wasn't what I called it. I didn't state, "I will be an entrepreneur." I didn't even know the term. What I did know was that I needed room. I needed to get away from individuals who told me who I should become. I wanted to experience the world, not read about it. I wanted risk. I wanted movement. I wanted to travel so far from everything that when I turned around, I could see things in focus.

That's why I went into shipping. It wasn't something that fascinated me as a child. It wasn't a family business. It was an escape. And it was concealed ambition. A passport to the world. A life where I didn't have to conform to the standard template. I went into shipping because it provided scope. And it required discipline.

Entering T.S. Chanakya was a victory in itself. It was not just about books; it was about breaking away from the weight of expectations. About pushing myself into a new setting. About showing that I could last in places where they did not hold back for you to get up to their level.

Chanakya was not some run-of-the-mill college. We weren't coddled. We were tempered. Right from the very beginning, everything there was meant to take away comfort and give in return is strength. Uniforms, drilling, and demerits, it was more of a boot camp than a learning space. But amidst the austerity, I gained clarity.

I was among the great minds. Young men who could answer difficult equations within minutes, who were brought up in elitist schools, who knew English with ease, without even realizing it. For a person like me, who had grown up in a smaller town and a life of contradictions, this was a new war front.

But I didn't blink. Intelligence didn't scare me. I possessed something else: flexibility. Perseverance. Emotional intelligence. I could read people as others read books. I could feel tension before it escalated into conflict. I could lead when others held back. That became my strength.

I remember a specific voyage near the Suez Canal when a storm caught us off guard. The ship didn't falter, but the crew did. A junior cadet, fresh, eager, and utterly terrified, froze at the ballast controls. The louder others shouted, the more paralyzed he became. That's when I stepped in. No shouting. No panic.

I placed my hand on his shoulder and said, "Look at me. Not the alarms. We're okay." Slowly, I walked him through the steps, calmly, clearly, without judgment. He did exactly what was needed.

Later that evening, he came to me and said, "Sir, I didn't panic because you didn't." That stuck with me. Fear is viral. But so is composure. When you hold your ground, even the unsure can borrow that steadiness.

It taught me something deeper: In chaos, people don't follow your rank, they follow your calm.

Going back to my days as a cadet, I wasn't the best of them. I missed lectures. I lived hard. I disobeyed the rules, then corrected them. I laughed loudly, lived freely, and rebelled against every norm. But beneath all that disorder, I was learning everything. The mechanics of vessels. The psychology of teams. The fine balance between discipline and morale.

And in the midst of all the troublemaking, I started growing. I understood that leadership did not include bellowing commands. It involved being cool in the storm. Listening more than you talk. Taking ownership without expecting praise. The boat did not worry about your grades. It was concerned about your attitude.

I remember an incident from my early days on board a ship. One night, mid-patrol in rough seas, our engine room reported an irregular vibration. The Chief was resting, and most officers were busy with routine checks. As the youngest officer on board, I was expected to report it up the chain and stay out of the way. But something in me didn't sit right. I had seen enough to know that engine vibrations aren't noise; they're warnings. I went down myself.

As I climbed into the heat and noise, I spotted it. One of the pump mountings had come loose. If left unattended, it would have escalated into a full-scale breakdown. I didn't panic. I gathered a small team, took the call to slow down the vessel, and we secured it in time.

When the Chief finally came in, he didn't yell. He just looked at me and nodded. That nod meant everything. That was the first time I truly understood leadership isn't about barking orders; it's about noticing before others, acting without fanfare, and holding the room without noise.

It was at university that I really began to become the person I would come to be known as. The contradictions were still there, I was still the wild card, still the activist with an agenda. But something had changed. There was more drive now. More hunger. More cuttingness in the way I perceived the world.

I noticed that whereas everybody was concerned about grades, hardly anybody was concerned about growth. Everybody was studying for exams. I was studying for life. I did not have a plan. But I had clarity. I wanted to create something of my own. I did not know what yet. But I knew why. I had tasted autonomy. I had learned to function without a safety net. And I enjoyed it.

What amazed everybody was that I didn't fall apart in crisis. I actually played better. The closer the call, the more focused I got. That skill at staying calm when the whole world was burning served me in my later years as my best tool. And it began there, in those cramped cabins and cacophonous engine rooms, where nobody else was going to rescue you but you.

When I entered ship life and graduated, it was just as I dreamed it, hard, unyielding, and exhilarating. The sea does not reward ego. It rewards being present. You repair the broken things. You lead when all things fall apart. You do what you have to do, even with shaking hands.

Each day was a new test. A new challenge. And I kept passing, not only because I was trained, but because I was built for it. Built after years of watching, learning, and shouldering more than my share of the burden.

But all of that came afterwards. The true foundation, the mentality, the resilience, the drive, had been formed much sooner. During those family meals when I saw others parade their achievements. During those moments of silent shame, when I knew we weren't failing, but we weren't succeeding either. During those fights on the streets, those rumors of comparisons, those afternoons spent being underestimated. All of that chiseled something in me that no textbook could.

And all the while, the voice within me continued to get louder.

Not yet.

Not yet.

Not this.

Not here.

That voice didn't scream. It whispered. And then one day, it roared.

That voice had no form, no identity. It wasn't urging me to be rich or famous. It was urging me to be more. Not for the benefit of applause, not to prove myself to anyone, but because I could sense, at a deep level, that I hadn't even begun to scratch the surface of what I was capable of.

By the time I had spent enough time on ships, that voice had matured. It wasn’t just rebellion anymore. It was quiet certainty. I had learned how to live in systems that weren’t designed for me. I had learned to lead when others waited to be told what to do. I had learned to trust my instincts, whether navigating a machine malfunction at midnight or dealing with an international crew that didn’t speak my language.

On one of my last voyages, the crew comprised men from four countries, each with their own rhythm, dialect, and culture. There were more miscommunications in an hour than most teams faced in a month. But when a crane jammed during a critical port operation, we didn't have the luxury of translators. We had a problem to solve.

I didn't issue orders. I moved. I pointed, explained with gestures, drew quick diagrams, and most importantly, stayed present. Everyone followed. The problem got solved.

Later that night, during dinner, one of the quietest crewmen raised his cup and said, in broken English, "To sir… who speaks with heart. Not only English."

That moment defined a truth I carry to this day: You don't need a loud voice to be heard. You need clarity. You need care. And when you lead with those, language stops being a barrier; it becomes a bridge.

But if I work it all back, none of that began at sea.

It began much sooner.

It began in those uncomfortable years, sitting across from tables where uncles talked about returns on real estate investments while I glared at my plate. It began in the look of relatives who smiled politely but never inquired as to what I was going to do with my life. It began with the rumble of that new car engine, parked out in front of our homestead, as the whole table went quiet, not because anyone had spoken, but because everyone knew everything.

That silence spoke louder than any insult.

And that silence defined me.

In a world where individuals wish to be moved by sensational rags-to-riches tales, I am from another trajectory. I didn't grow up with nothing. I had something growing up, but always just short of plenty. And that "just short" sensation does a very particular thing to you. It doesn't make you angry. It makes you precise. You start to measure your effort. You start to plan your moments. You start to see gaps between timing and value, between scarcity and opportunity, between what people say and what they really need.

That mentality is what formed the foundation of all the businesses I went on to create. But way before I was even considering revenue or size, I was learning to read people. To read moments. To listen to my instincts even when all the paperwork indicated no. That self-awareness did not come from books. It came from living in a tier-two world with tier-one aspirations.

And here's something I never admit, but must be said.

There were times I questioned everything.

There were times I glanced at the system in front of me, the safe ones who played it safe, abided by the rules, joined civil services, married early, settled into security, and wondered if I was the stupid one. Perhaps they were correct. Perhaps this burning within me was a miscalculation. Perhaps I was searching for something that did not exist.

But then something small would occur. Something I had done would pay off. Something I had risked would come through. A door would open up. And I'd be reminded again why I did what I did in the first place. Not for accolades. Not even for a reward. But for alignment.

I wasn't trying to cut away from my beginnings. I was trying to stretch out from them.

I never resented where I was from. I just simply did not let it dictate where I could go. My drive wasn't created out of a lack. It was created out of proximity to more. Out of watching people live bigger, better, and fuller lives, and wondering how that wasn't an option for me as well.

What the world doesn't realize is that the greatest resistance is not from enemies. It is from proximity. From those who claim to love you but secretly want you to shrink. From systems that pay to be safe and penalize drive. From old people who love you but cut your wings before they have seen you soar.

I had to resist everything.

Not with an argument. Not with revolt. But with outcomes.

I had to demonstrate, over and over again, that my decisions weren't careless, they were deliberate. That my risks weren't reckless, they were planned. That my hunger wasn't ego, it was intent.

And that takes time.

Sometimes years.

Sometimes a lifetime.

There is no grand finale to this chapter of my life. No one perfect moment where I stood atop a mountain and shouted out that I had arrived. Because I hadn't. I was still so far from anything. I was still raw. Still in the process of forming. Still daydreaming.

But what had shifted, on a fundamental level, was that I no longer doubted the flame within me.

I no longer questioned whether I was mistaken for yearning more.

I knew I wasn't.

Because by then, I had lived enough, led enough, and lost enough to know one thing that would see me through all that came next:

You don't need a map.

You just need a reason.

And mine had been tempered in silence, made stronger in resistance, and energized by a vision that refused to perish.

Chapter 2: The Employee Decade - Learning in the Trenches

"The sea doesn't forgive pretenders. Onboard a ship, there's no space for borrowed confidence or theoretical competence. Either you learn fast, or you become a liability.

I didn't step into my first job thinking I'd master it. I stepped in knowing I'd have to survive it first."

When I started on my first ship as a Junior Officer, I was full of the youth's arrogance and the hunger of one who had something to prove. I had worked hard, trained hard, and told myself that I knew everything. No textbook can inform you of the brutal realities of salt-covered steel decks, middle-of-the-night emergencies, and a multiracial crew running on adrenaline and discipline. In theory, I was prepared. Practically at sea, I was green.

I vividly remember my first evening aboard. Engines growled like a beast alive beneath the deck. Corridors smelled of oil, rust, and memories. My cabin was as tiny as the average bathroom, but with a porthole that gave more movement than view. I sat on the edge of the bunk, holding the railing with one hand to keep myself steady. My other hand held the schedule for the next day, watch duty at 0400. There was no one to complain to. No onboarding manager. No HR welcome kit. Just the silence of water below and the weight of expectation above.

The first few months were brutal. Every mistake was visible. Every hesitation magnified. There was no room to disappear. You either showed up or you got someone hurt. That's how tightly interlocked ship life was. If one person slacked, everyone paid.

I cleaned rusted pipelines, wiped engine room floors, and checked pressure gauges in sweltering heat. At the time, it felt like punishment. Later, I understood it was precision training. Every screw had its significance. Every alarm had a history. And every decision, even one made at 2 AM in silence, carried consequences.

The hierarchy was clear but not always kind. Orders came fast, and so did the judgment. But slowly, I found my rhythm. Not because I was the strongest or the smartest, but because I was observant. I learned to watch how people moved, how they delegated, how they responded to tension. Leadership, I discovered, wasn't always loud. Often, it was the person who didn't flinch when others did.

By my third voyage, I had become the one people came to for small answers. And slowly, those small answers added up. I wasn't just a Junior Officer anymore. I was dependable. It wasn't a promotion. It was a shift in perception.

One night during rough weather, the radar system glitched. Visibility dropped. The crew on duty froze for a few seconds. I was technically off-watch, but I was nearby and stepped in. I didn't bark orders. I didn't pretend to know everything. I just took charge of what I did know: manual plotting, calm communication, quick checks. We stabilized within minutes. No panic. No incident. Just trust earned in silence.

Those moments taught me more than any leadership seminar could. The sea didn't reward talk. It rewarded presence.

With time, I began climbing the ranks: third mate, second mate, chief officer. Each step meant more responsibility, but also more insight. I started understanding the human engine behind the mechanical one. A ship functioned not just because of engineering, but because of psychology. Cultural misunderstandings, fatigue, and family problems, these didn't show up in engine logs, but they decided how the crew performed.

There were tensions, always. Miscommunications that sparked flare-ups, hierarchies that felt like prisons. But within all that, I learned how to manage people, not just by giving instructions, but by managing energy, emotion, and expectation.

At 27, I became one of the youngest captains in the fleet.

It should have felt like a peak. In some ways, it did. The uniform carried weight. The respect was real. And yet, something had shifted in me. The work was fulfilling, but I began feeling a pull I couldn't explain, a sense that I was learning in a straight line, but growing in a circle. Repeating, refining, but not expanding.

Still, I stayed. Because leaving a ship doesn't just mean changing your job. It means changing your rhythm. At sea, you sleep with waves and wake with radar scans. You don't chase promotions, you chase safe berths. You don't think in quarters, you think in voyages.

But eventually, the itch became too loud to ignore. I had started to see patterns, not just in the tides, but in how leadership played out across cultures, crews, and companies. I realized that the same issues I saw on ships, unclear communication, misplaced accountability, and egos disguised as expertise, existed everywhere. The difference was that ships couldn't afford to ignore them.

That's when I decided to come ashore.

My first corporate job felt like a culture shock. The office had air conditioning, ergonomic chairs, and coffee machines. But it also had something I hadn't expected: politics. Meetings for meetings' sake. Reports written more for optics than outcomes. Promotions driven more by perception than performance.

I was used to urgency having a reason. Here, it often felt manufactured. There were ten-step approval chains for decisions that took five minutes at sea. I struggled, not because I couldn't adapt, but because I couldn't understand why things were designed this way.

And yet, I learned.

I learned how organizations functioned. I watched how systems were built, how people maneuvered through ambiguity, and how leadership looked from boardrooms instead of bridges. I started noting how few people truly felt seen at work. How many operated from fear, not ownership. It reminded me of vessels running on emergency power, technically afloat, but vulnerable to the next storm.

In my early roles, I was assigned to crisis operations, vessels in trouble, contracts gone wrong, and compliance red flags. It was as if my sea background made me a natural firefighter. And I took to it. I thrived under pressure. Not because I liked chaos, but because I hated confusion.

In one company, a vessel had collided in port. No injuries, no pollution, but the media had caught wind of it. Internally, panic spread. Executives blamed each other. Managers scrambled for answers. I stepped in, not as the most senior person, but as the calmest. I initiated emergency protocols, drafted the first press statement, coordinated with local authorities, and stabilized the situation within forty-eight hours. When the dust settled, no one remembered my designation. They remembered my response.

That became a pattern.

I wasn't the loudest in the room, but people began turning to me when things got serious. I began mentoring junior managers. Not formally, just through conversations, debriefs, and listening. I asked them better questions. Sometimes, that's all people need.

But over time, that familiar restlessness returned. I began seeing the same problems repeat across companies, teams without cohesion, strategy without soul, growth without grounding. I wasn't disillusioned. I was awakening.

It was during this phase that I started asking myself different questions, not "What's my next role?" but "What's my role in all of this?"

I had entered employment to learn. To observe. To test myself. And I had done all of that. But now, I could feel the edges of the system pressing in.

When you've been trained by the sea, the land feels both safer and more slippery.

Corporate jobs didn't demand my survival, but they often tested my sense of self. In the early months ashore, I found myself recalibrating every instinct. At sea, directness was valued. On land, it was often seen as aggression. At sea, delay could mean disaster. In offices, delay was currency. A well-worded email could substitute for action, and presence in a meeting could be confused for progress.

I didn't complain. I studied.

I noticed how companies ran on unspoken rules, rituals, and relics. There were systems for everything, but the soul was in very few of them. Many professionals were technically skilled, but emotionally disengaged. The brightest minds spent half their energy on impression management and the other half on self-preservation.

What struck me most wasn't the inefficiency. It was the silence around it. People knew what wasn't working. But they adapted, not because they agreed, but because they were exhausted.

I joined multiple firms across this decade, never because I lacked opportunity, but because I chased understanding. I shifted across departments and industries. Each move was surgical. I was collecting data about processes, about hierarchies, about how things break and how they're fixed.

It was somewhere in the middle of all this movement between job switches, industry shifts, and growing clarity that Mridula entered my life. She didn't arrive like a dramatic plot twist. She arrived like a balance.

We met through a mutual connection in the maritime industry. Our conversations began over operations and audits, but slowly drifted toward books, childhood stories, and shared silences that didn't feel awkward. Where I moved fast, she moved with intention. Where I challenged everything, she measured things quietly before choosing her words.

She didn't just listen; she understood. And in a world where I was constantly analyzing people, she made me feel seen.

Marriage followed, not impulsively but with mutual clarity. I wouldn't say I was an easy man to live with. My schedules were erratic. My mind often occupied. I brought home not just fatigue, but the weight of the things I couldn't say in boardrooms. But Mridula absorbed it all, never trying to fix it, never asking for more than honesty.

My mother, sharp and commanding in her own right, took time to adjust. There were moments of tension; two strong women learning to orbit around the same sun. But slowly, something resembling friendship grew between them. They both knew I was flawed. They just loved me in different languages.

Looking back, that time grounded me more than any title. In Mridula, I didn't just find a partner. I found someone who reminded me, every single day, that being ambitious didn't mean forgetting how to be human.

At work, I became less interested in the promotion ladder and more focused on pattern recognition.

One role introduced me to compliance structures. Another put me knee-deep into commercial operations. Yet another gave me a crash course in procurement politics. Each job added a new lens. And every time I felt I had outgrown the view, I moved.

There was a stretch when I worked in a firm undergoing an internal audit crisis. Documentation was broken. Vendor records were chaotic. Policies looked good on paper but hadn't been practiced in months. The leadership team was defensive, the finance team terrified. I remember spending two straight weekends rewriting workflows from scratch, taking what I knew from sea checklists and adapting them to ground operations.

When the external auditors came, they pointed out lapses, but also noted the structure we had implemented. We weren't flawless, but we were now functional. That moment taught me something simple and profound: clarity reduces fear. When people know what to do, they stop worrying about what could go wrong.

But even clarity couldn't shield me from the cultural undercurrents. In one organization, I was part of a team that had just cracked a difficult operational target ahead of schedule. The numbers were undeniable. But in the leadership meeting that followed, credit flowed sideways. The loudest voice got the praise. The person who had led the final client negotiation wasn't even mentioned.

I sat quietly in that room and watched the show unfold. And I wrote just one line in my notebook that evening: *"Visibility and value are not the same. Learn the difference, but don't confuse them."*

There were many such notes, scattered across journals, saved in voice memos, sometimes scribbled on boarding passes. They weren't complaints. They were clues. Clues pointing to something deeper: I wasn't designed to only perform within systems. I was beginning to long to design them.

But before that realization crystallized, there was still work to do. Still lessons to learn.

A turning point came when I was assigned to lead an internal transformation project. The goal was to streamline the company's operations across three verticals. On the surface, it looked like a technical challenge: systems integration, data harmonization, process improvement. But within weeks, I realized the real challenge was people.

Departments operated like fiefdoms. Senior managers protected their turf. Meetings became war zones in polite clothing. Every suggestion felt like a threat to someone's legacy.

I decided to play the long game. I met each team leader one-on-one. Listened more than I spoke. Understood their fears, most of which had nothing to do with operations. They feared irrelevance. They feared loss of status. They feared being replaced by processes smarter than them.

Once I understood that, the work changed. We began co-creating processes instead of imposing them. We celebrated small wins publicly and corrected in private. The implementation was delayed, but successful. More importantly, it stayed in place long after I moved on.

That experience taught me a foundational truth: change doesn't begin with systems. It begins with safety. People don't resist change. They resist fear.

But not every company was ready for that kind of insight.

In one job, I pushed for the digitization of operations, proposed a pilot that could save the company both time and cost. I had data, case studies, and vendor proposals. The idea was quietly shelved. I later learned that a senior executive had lobbied against it, not because it wouldn't work, but because it would reduce his control.

That was the first time I felt a strange ache, not of disappointment, but of disconnection. I wasn't just fighting inefficiency. I was fighting inertia.

And yet, I didn't leave.

I stayed. I observed. I documented.

Because I had started seeing the corporate world for what it really was, a theatre. Some roles were scripted. Others were improvised. But most people didn't know who the audience was. And fewer still asked if the performance had meaning.

During this period, I also became a father.

Niranjan was born after a complicated pregnancy. I still remember the moment I held him for the first time, tiny, breathing, wrapped in soft cotton. In that instant, the world collapsed and expanded at once. I wasn't just a professional anymore. I was someone's reference point for love, strength, and time.

But the timing was unkind.

My job demanded more travel than ever. Weekly flights, quarterly reviews, and client visits that often stretched into weekends. I kept telling myself it was temporary. That I was building something important.

Until one night, Niranjan asked, "Why do you live in airports, Papa?"

That night, I didn't open my laptop. I opened my journal. And I wrote: "*If I keep winning outside but losing where it matters most, am I really winning?*"

Still, I continued. Because stopping isn't always an option when you carry the weight of legacy and the pressure of provision.

Thankfully, I wasn't alone. Mridula held the fort at home with a grace I couldn't have mustered. My mother remained the emotional engine, filling gaps I didn't even know existed. Together, they created a world that allowed me to fly. But every flight came with its own cost. The guilt began to compound, not dramatically, but quietly. Like background noise that never turned off.

Professionally, I was succeeding. I was now in strategic roles, sitting in meetings where capital was discussed, where futures were shaped. But increasingly, I began to feel like a visitor. Like someone who was welcome but never fully home.

There was one particular evening that sealed the sentiment. I had presented a comprehensive proposal to integrate our maritime operations with a digital monitoring solution. The pilot had worked. The cost-benefit was undeniable. My presentation had been well-received, on the surface.

Later that evening, over drinks, a senior leader leaned over and said, "You think like an owner, not like an employee. That's dangerous."

He meant it as a caution. But for me, it was confirmation.

He was right.

I didn't belong to the system anymore.

But I wasn't angry.

I was ready.

I didn't leave immediately after that comment. I stayed. Months passed. Meetings came and went. Titles changed. But something inside me had begun to shift. A quiet detachment had taken root. Not bitterness, just a kind of inner stillness that refused to be stirred by performance reviews or KPIs anymore.

The external signs were still positive. My department was hitting its numbers. Clients were happy. I had even been invited to join a task force for restructuring a critical business vertical. But I had started reading the room differently. The metrics didn't move me anymore. What caught my attention now were things others overlooked, the invisible morale drops, the performative praise, the good people quietly burning out while carrying the company on their shoulders.

I began spending more time listening, really listening. Colleagues confided things they'd never said in open forums. Stories of exhaustion, of being passed over, of putting in years without so much as a genuine acknowledgment. They didn't want perks. They wanted presence. They didn't need a new HR policy. They needed leadership that felt human.

At times, I found myself being that presence. I mentored juniors not because it was expected, but because it made the job feel real again. I had team members who came to me with more than work, career doubts, family struggles, and existential questions about purpose. I never had all the answers. But I made sure they left with one thing: clarity. Even if it was temporary.

It was in these moments that I found meaning, far more than I ever did in bonus letters or slide decks. I still remember a young analyst, brilliant, insecure, and overwhelmed. She was considering quitting, convinced she wasn't cut out for corporate life. I spent an hour with her one Friday evening. We didn't talk about deliverables. We talked about resilience. About how doubt doesn't mean you're broken, it just means you're awake.

She didn't quit. Two years on, she was managing a multi-million-dollar change project. When she texted me with a photo from her new Singapore office, I grinned, not proudly, but because I felt productive.

But utility, I was realizing, was not sufficient.

Something deeper was stirring. Not a dream, not yet. Just discomfort. The sense that I was living with one foot on the shore and one foot in the water, neither anchored nor sailing. I was growing, yes. But the growth felt horizontal. Sideways. Safe.

There's a specific kind of fatigue that comes not from overwork, but from under-purpose. I was tired. Not because I was doing too much. But because I wasn't doing what felt most aligned. I was meeting expectations. But they weren't mine.

The final years of that decade blurred together, a mix of new roles, bigger mandates, and increasing responsibility. I moved across verticals: strategy, procurement, and legal compliance.

I wasn't being boxed into a domain, and that gave me the space to study how organizations truly functioned from end to end. But it also gave me more evidence of how fractured they often were.

In one project, I was asked to clean up a post-merger integration. Two firms had combined under the promise of synergy, but culturally, they were oil and water. Departments duplicated work. Clients received contradictory communication. Internal teams were unsure who reported to whom. On paper, it was a merger. In spirit, it was a silent war.

My job was to align the chaos. I approached it like a sea operation, first, understand the crew. Who's threatened? Who's confused? Who's pretending they're fine but silently looking for the exit?

It took months. Not just of planning, but of patience. We eventually turned it around, not because we had the best systems, but because we began telling the truth. We acknowledged what was broken, invited people to co-design the fix, and showed that vulnerability wasn't weakness, it was trust.

That project became a case study in quiet leadership. But it also cemented what I already knew: most problems in business aren't technical. They're emotional. And most leaders don't fail because they don't know what to do. They fail because they don't know how to be.

Outside the office, life was evolving too. Niranjan was growing fast, faster than I could keep up with. His questions were getting more complex. His eyes more observant. There were weekends when we'd go for a walk, and he'd casually say something that would hit me harder than any corporate review.

“Why are you always reading work stuff?” he asked once. “Don’t you know enough already?”

I wanted to say, “I’m learning so I can grow.”

But I paused.

Because the real answer was more uncomfortable.

I was still reading to stay ahead of something I couldn’t name. To keep the engine running. To prove to myself that I was still moving. Still evolving. Still valuable.

But I had begun to wonder: at what point does learning become hiding?

Around this time, I started waking up earlier. Not to work. To think. I’d sit in the quiet, before the house stirred, and just breathe. No screens. No emails. Just pen, paper, and presence. The thoughts weren’t dramatic. They were simple. But they kept returning.

What if this isn’t all there is? What if I’ve been preparing for something else, something that hasn’t yet taken shape?

I wasn’t dissatisfied with my job. I respected my colleagues. I had learned more than I could have ever imagined when I first started out. But I also knew that respect isn’t the same as resonance. And I had reached a point where I craved the latter.

There was one moment, in particular, that clarified everything.

It was during an off-site leadership retreat. We had all been asked to write down what we wanted our legacy to be, in one sentence. A seemingly simple task.

Around the room, people wrote things like "Leave a mark on the industry," "Drive innovation in my domain," or "Become a global leader in my field."

I wrote: "*To create something where people feel seen.*"

That evening, as I read my own words again, something clicked.

I wasn't built to climb ladders. I was built to build spaces.

That was my truth.

But I didn't quit that day.

Because sometimes clarity doesn't demand a decision. It demands attention.

So I gave it mine.

I didn't talk about it. I didn't ask for feedback. I just kept showing up, with a new awareness. I started observing the world through a different lens. Not as a performer, but as a potential creator.

I had no business plan. No investor meetings. No branding concepts.

But I had something stronger.

Readiness.

The kind that comes after years of friction, observation, and quiet resistance. The kind that doesn't scream, but whispers: It's time.

Not to leap.

But to listen.

Because before every bold move comes the silence that makes it possible.

And in that silence, something had begun to take root.

I once believed that work was a stepping stone. That you transition from one job to the next, each a step on some unseen ladder that brought you closer to the life you desired. But at some point during those ten years, I came to understand something more profound: work is reflective. It mirrors what you hold important, what you struggle against, what you accept, and more importantly, who you are becoming.

The decade I spent in employment was not just about work. It was about exposure. Not to titles or industries, but to human behavior in all its rawness, ego and empathy, ambition and fear, politics and potential.

I worked with leaders who inspired me and others who taught me what not to become. I saw how silence in meetings often said more than the loudest voice. I watched people shrink in the face of authority, and others blossom under trust. I observed how organizations repeated the same dysfunctions across sectors, each thinking their problems were unique.

And I paid attention.

More than the money, more than the positions, it was these insights that shaped me. They taught me that leadership is less about control and more about clarity. That systems without empathy break down even when they perform. That culture is not a poster on the wall; it's the energy in the room when no one's watching.

By the ninth year, I had stopped thinking of myself as an employee. Not out of arrogance. Out of misfit honesty. I was still inside the system, still delivering, still leading. But I had begun thinking like an outsider. I couldn't stop noticing what was broken. I couldn't stop imagining how things could be different. I wasn't rebelling, I was evolving.

The shift wasn't external. There was no confrontation. No resignation email drafted in frustration. I still showed up. Still smiled. Still solved problems. But the way I processed those problems had changed. I no longer asked, "How can I fix this?" I began asking, "Why does this keep happening?" And slowly, "What would I do differently if I could build this from scratch?"

That's how it starts.

Not with an idea, but with a question that won't go away.

I didn't resent employment. I respected it. It gave me a front-row seat to how the world operates. It paid for my early mistakes. It built my discipline. It refined my instincts. Most of all, it gave me stakes. People. Relationships. Consequences.

Without that decade, I would have started from the surface. Because of it, I was building from the core.

And yet, by the end of it, I was no longer willing to trade time for security. Not because I had enough money. But because I had enough clarity. I knew that staying another five years would not bring new wisdom, only new ways of rationalizing comfort.

The turning point wasn't dramatic. It was cumulative.

It came in glances, when a junior came to me in tears after being overlooked for credit. When I sat through meetings where strategy was diluted to suit egos. When I caught myself nodding at decisions I knew were flawed just to preserve harmony.

It came in my journal entries, shorter, sharper, more restless.

It came in Niranjan's silences, when I missed a school performance, and he didn't even mention it later. Not out of forgiveness, but resignation.

And it came in the quietest moments. Early mornings when the house was asleep, and I found myself staring at a blank page, wondering: What if I don't write a new script? What if I just end up editing this one for the rest of my life?

Those questions became the compass.

I didn't have answers. But I had direction.

That's what the employee decade gave me. Not a career. A compass.

It taught me that growth is not about climbing. It's about seeing. Seeing who you are in the face of systems that try to define you. Seeing what you choose to protect, your reputation, or your voice. Seeing which parts of yourself expand under pressure, and which parts shrink.

And once you've seen enough, you can't unsee it.

That's when you know: it's time to stop watching the machine and start building something of your own.

But you don't leap immediately.

You sit with the weight of what you've seen. You give thanks for what served you. You forgive what didn't. And you begin to imagine, not wildly, but wisely.

Because when you've spent a decade learning what doesn't work, you carry a blueprint for something that just might.

And that's where the real story begins.

Not in the leap.

But in the stillness before it.

Chapter 3: The Leap from Job Security to Business Risk

"You don't leave a good job because it's unbearable. You leave it because something greater is calling."

When I finally stepped away, it wasn't from frustration or failure. It was from the top floor. I was already in a senior leadership role. Respected. Trusted. Poised for elevation to Group CEO in due course. Many assumed it was only a matter of time. Some even said, "Just stay the course. The title is yours."

But titles were never the goal. I wasn't chasing a chair. I was chasing clarity.

The systems I was a part of had shaped me, tested me, and rewarded me. But they also began to echo. The same meetings, the same metrics, the same polished narratives that rarely touched the deeper problems. And somewhere between boardrooms and balance sheets, something inside me started asking: What if the next chapter wasn't about climbing further, but building something from the ground up?

That seed took root quietly.

One evening, returning home from a long regional review trip, I found Niranjan sketching at the table. "It's our house," he said. I smiled until I realized I wasn't in it.

I looked at the sketch. He had drawn Mridula, my mother, and himself. Even the neighbor's dog. But not me.

That night, I couldn't sleep.

Because somewhere between loyalty to the job and responsibility to my family, I had become a visitor in my own life. And once you see that clearly, you can't unsee it.

That drawing wasn't a complaint. It was a reflection. I had been present everywhere except in the moments that mattered most. That wasn't a failure. That was misalignment. A sign that something needed to shift, not because I was falling behind, but because I was no longer walking in the same direction.

I didn't act hastily. I never do. I began writing, drafting, observing, not resignation letters, but models, ideas, frameworks.

At first, it was a series of frustrations. Things I had seen broken in companies. Bottlenecks in operations. Gaps in compliance. Missed signals in client relationships. The kind of things no one noticed because they were hidden between departments.

Then it became outlines. What if there were a system that tied these loose ends together? Not a consultancy, but an execution model. Not a theory, but a service engine that could operate with the rigor of a ship, but the fluidity of a human team.

I wasn't sure what it would become. I only knew what it shouldn't be, a copy of everything I was leaving behind.

The insight came not from emotion, but from exposure: I saw a persistent flaw across companies - strong strategies, weak execution. High-level vision, low-level commitment. No one was solving that gap with consistency or care.

Mridula noticed the shift. I was quieter. Less reactive. More distant, sometimes. She didn't pry. But one night, as we sat on the balcony sipping chai, she said, "You're carrying something heavy. If you don't speak it, it will speak for you."

I told her everything. Not as a pitch, but as a confession.

She didn't interrupt. She didn't ask for timelines or business plans. She just asked one question: "Do you want to build this because you hate what exists, or because you believe in what could be?"

I took a long breath before answering.

"Both," I said. "But mostly the second."

That conversation changed something. Not externally. I was still going to work the next day. But internally, a line had been crossed. I wasn't waiting for permission anymore. I was preparing for a departure.

In the months that followed, I began operating on two tracks. By day, I continued my role, closing deals, managing teams, and executing strategy. By night, I built what would become Aethon.

It didn't have a name yet. Just a notebook full of scribbles, models, flowcharts, and quotes I clipped from articles. But the soul was clear, it would be a company that put execution before ego, people before pitch decks, and integrity before positioning.

I started reaching out to old colleagues, not to recruit, but to sense-check. I spoke to suppliers I respected. Asked them what they hated most about working with clients. I asked junior professionals what they wished their managers understood. I asked clients what felt like missing even when a job was "technically complete."

The answers were raw. And revealing.

Most of what was broken wasn't technical. It was relational. People felt unseen. Systems felt rigid. Trust was brittle. And in that vacuum, mediocrity had become the default setting.

I saw an opportunity. Not a market gap. A human gap.

I began preparing. I built a 12-month runway, not for capital (I already had that), but for clarity. Then, I began testing. I took on small consulting assignments on weekends. Helped a friend's company with an audit restructuring. Advised a start-up on process mapping. Each time, I observed my own energy. Did I feel drained? Or did I feel alive?

The answer came easily.

I felt like myself again.

It's strange how clarity doesn't always feel liberating at first. Sometimes it feels like a burden. The more I became sure that I had to leave, the heavier each day at work began to feel.

The same boardrooms I once entered with purpose now felt like spaces I was borrowing time in. The strategies I once drove began to sound hollow in my own ears. I was no longer solving the same problems; I was replaying the same patterns.

I knew I had to leave. So, I did, even when my CFO tried getting back at me by holding up my bank clearance. Probably, he was scared of my financial background, or probably, he didn't want me to leave, but I knew my decision, and I stood by it.

When my CFO tried to hold my release and clearance, I had a heated argument with him, told him that it was not about the money for me, that my salary for the past two or three years was lying in that bank account, untouched, making it clear to him that money did not matter the least bit. It was the purpose that mattered to me. So, if he tries to hold my release and clearance, it will not happen without me coming in for a showdown. He knew I was serious and that stopping me was not an option for him anymore.

I finally exited the corporate world only to create one of my own.

With solid investments, successful side ventures, and no financial pressure, this wasn't a risky leap. It was a conscious pivot. A return to building, not out of necessity, but out of purpose. Because when you're already in line for the top, the real question isn't what you're leaving behind. It's what you're making room for.

I registered the company, Aethon.

One of my sharpest executives, someone I deeply respected and had mentored, came up with the name: Aethon, the burning horse that pulls the chariot of the sun. It felt right. Not just symbolically, but spiritually. It captured what I envisioned: a firm that moved with discipline, fire, and soul.

The business idea wasn't born out of dissatisfaction. It was born out of responsibility. I wasn't escaping something broken. I was building something better. The idea was simple, but radical in its honesty: we wouldn't chase contracts; we'd solve problems. We wouldn't posture; we'd partner. We wouldn't scale blindly; we'd grow mindfully.

Aethon wasn't a rebellion against the corporate system. It was a responsibility I chose to solve problems others ignored, to build something that would outlive titles, and to lead in a way that felt true.

And even though the world saw it as a step away from power, I knew it was the first real step toward mine.

The first few days after leaving were oddly quiet.

No calendar. No flights. No urgent calls.

I remember waking up on Monday and just sitting with a blank notepad, not because I had nothing to do, but because I could choose what to do.

That freedom is both beautiful and terrifying.

There's no applause for leaving a stable job. No standing ovation for chasing your own dream. Just silence. And spreadsheets.

The first few weeks were spent turning thoughts into execution.

I finalised the website. Built a pitch deck, not for investors, but for myself. I needed to see what I stood for. I wrote down our philosophy in big letters across the wall of my home study: We don't sell services. We deliver trust.

I rented a small co-working desk. It was nothing fancy. Just a table, a whiteboard, and access to a shared conference room. But it felt like the beginning of something sacred.

Aethon's earliest proposals were handwritten. The first logo was designed on a basic graphic tool. The legal templates were borrowed and modified. There was no team yet. Just me, my phone, and a list of people I believed I could serve better than anyone else.

I started reaching out, not with a sales pitch, but with a question:

"What's one operational headache that no one is solving for you?"

Most people were surprised.

"Is this a sales call?"

"No," I'd say. "This is a design conversation."

Some hung up. Some laughed. But a few listened. In fact, they didn't just listen; they felt what I was saying.

Those few became the first clients.

The first contract I landed was for a mid-sized marine operator. They were struggling with vessel inspection protocols. I had written a framework for that exact issue two years ago, just never got to implement it.

I pulled it out. Polished it. Presented it.

We signed the deal.

It wasn't large. But it was real.

I remember walking out of their office and sitting in my car, staring at the dashboard, whispering under my breath:

"This is how it begins."

The second project came through a former colleague, compliance structuring for an offshore project. Again, nothing glamorous. But we delivered it in record time. And word began to spread.

I hired my first part-time analyst. Then, a project coordinator. We operated lean. Efficient. Every rupee was tracked. Every client call was logged. Every piece of feedback was studied.

We weren't trying to look big.

We were trying to be useful.

That became our metric: Did we matter to the people we served?

And in those early months, as I drove across the city for meetings, proposals, and coffee chats, I began to feel something I hadn't in years.

Alignment.

Not excitement. Not adrenaline. Just a deep, daily sense of doing what I was meant to.

People think the hardest part of starting a company is capital. It's not. It's conviction. Capital helps you move. Conviction tells you where.

In those early months, I was spending more time on culture than on revenue. Not because I didn't need the money, I did. But because I knew that if the foundation was wrong, no amount of billing would save us.

So I obsessed over the small things. Our proposal format. Our tone in emails. The way we documented meetings. Every piece of output was a signal. Not just to clients, but to ourselves, this is who we are. We don't take shortcuts. We don't dress up failures. We don't act bigger than we are.

And slowly, that posture began to attract people.

People who were tired of corporate hypocrisy. Smart, driven, honest professionals who wanted to work hard, but without pretending. Some came part-time. Others offered to freelance. A few just dropped in to say, “Let me know when you’re hiring full-time.”

I didn’t promise anyone a ladder. I promised them space.

Space to do real work. To be heard. To be held to a high standard without being made to feel small.

Our office was still a co-working space. Our systems were still evolving. But the energy was different. People stayed late not because of policy, but because they cared. We celebrated small wins, a signed retainer, a good feedback mail, and a client call that ended in laughter.

It felt alive.

And then, just as we were hitting our stride, life hit back.

It started with fatigue. Not the usual kind. This was different. My speech began slurring slightly. One morning, while brushing my teeth, I noticed the right side of my face wasn’t moving. I tried to smile. Only half responded.

I knew something was wrong.

The diagnosis came quickly: Bell’s Palsy. A temporary facial paralysis. Stress-induced. Common, they said. Recoverable. But these words and reassurance do not help when you cannot recognize the person you look at in the mirror.

I had built my identity around strength, sharpness, and presence. And now, I felt like I had no control. Words stumbled out. My eye wouldn’t close fully. I could still think, work, and decide, but I didn’t feel like myself.

And to complicate it all, Kamakshi was born around the same time.

Her arrival should've been the highlight of our year. The softness that wrapped all the sharp edges of life in something sacred.

She was born healthy. Quiet. Wide-eyed. The only girl in our extended family. She didn't cry much. She just watched, like she already knew more than we did.

I held her once.

Then flew out two days later for a client pitch.

Even now, I struggle to explain how that felt. Like I was holding everything and nothing at once.

Mridula didn't complain. Not once. She knew the stakes. Knew that this wasn't a company built from luxury, it was built from need. But that didn't make the leaving easier.

I remember being in a hotel lobby in Singapore, prepping for a client presentation, and glancing at a photo of Kamakshi on my phone. She was barely a week old. I stared at her for a full minute, then turned the phone over. I couldn't handle the ache.

The pitch went well.

But I don't remember the client's name.

What I do remember is the moment after, sitting in my room, lights off, face still half-paralyzed, wondering if this was what I left stability for.

Was I building something meaningful, or just replacing one treadmill with another?

That question haunted me for weeks.

But I kept working. Not because I was suppressing the fear, but because I was working through it.

I reduced my travel. Delegated more. Started walking slower. Sleeping deeper. Hugging Niranjan longer. Holding Kamakshi without looking at my phone.

And something strange happened.

Aethon didn't slow down.

It became sharper.

Our proposals became tighter. Our delivery stronger. Our client relationships warmer. Because I wasn't chasing outcomes anymore. I was anchoring in values.

That period, difficult as it was, taught me two things.

First: You're never building just a business. You're building a mirror. It will reflect your energy, no matter how well you disguise it.

Second: Purpose is not found in the launch. It's found in the questions you ask when everything feels broken.

In the quiet of those weeks, between physiotherapy sessions and late-night feeds, I found my answer.

I wasn't building Aethon to escape employment.

I was building it to return. To myself. To a way of working that honored people, not just profit. To a life where integrity wasn't a choice, it was the default setting.

One morning, months into recovery, I stood in front of the mirror and smiled.

Not a full smile, just a twitch on both sides.

But it was enough.

Enough to tell me that I was back. Not fully. But deeply.

And from that point on, we stopped being a startup.

We became a movement.

Somewhere in that second year, Aethon stopped being my project and started becoming my identity. Aethon wasn't the only thing that found its rhythm. Alongside the other ventures I had long nurtured, especially real estate, began to take deeper root. Real estate wasn't new for me; I had been dabbling in it from my early years. But now, with greater clarity and resources, it evolved into something more intentional: development projects, partnerships, and structured ventures. What once felt like side hustles were now serious, thriving extensions of the same spirit I had poured into Aethon: build with integrity, grow with consistency, and leave a mark that lasts beyond transactions.

It didn't happen on a big milestone. Not with a massive contract. Not with an article in a trade journal or a standing ovation at some industry event. It happened, as most true things do, in silence.

I was sitting with a junior analyst we had just hired. She was young, bright, and nervous. It was her second week. We had just finished a client debrief and were packing up when she turned to me and said, "Sir, is it okay if I suggest a different way to structure tomorrow's deck? I think we're explaining too much before we get to the value."

I smiled.

Not because her observation was sharp. But because she felt safe enough to say it.

That was the moment I knew we were building the right culture. When people don't just work for you, but with you. When they know they can disagree with you and not be diminished. That's when a company begins to breathe on its own.

In the months that followed, we began to attract more clients, not through outbound hustle, but through inbound referrals. "You guys don't overcomplicate things." "Your team listens." "You're the first vendor who speaks like a partner." These were the compliments we collected. More valuable than any testimonial.

We didn't have a business development team. We had conversations.

We didn't pitch. We presented possibilities.

And we didn't try to sound smarter than we were. We simply told the truth, clearly, consistently, and without frills.

I still remember one client in particular. A medium-sized logistics firm that had been struggling with vendor integration. We didn't offer them a glossy solution. We sat with their operations team, mapped their chaos manually, and proposed a boring but bulletproof approach. They agreed. Two months later, their CEO called and said, "You saved us six months of mistakes. I've never been more grateful for boring."

That's when I wrote a note on the whiteboard in our new (still small) office:

"Our job is not to impress. Our job is to work."

That line became part of our onboarding material.

And while the company took shape externally, something quieter was happening internally.

I had begun to change.

I was no longer driven by proving anything. Not to the industry. Not to former colleagues. Not to clients. And not to myself. The hunger was still there. But it had transformed. From proving to improving. It didn't happen overnight. Instead, it happened after something Mridula had said.

As I look back, I remember that we had shifted homes multiple times over the years. I saw it as growth; each new house a reflection of the life we were building. To me, a well-designed home, a spacious office, and a reliable car, all within our means, were more than assets. They were silent indicators of trust, professionalism, and readiness. In the business world, appearances matter. A good space doesn't just reflect status; it signals stability.

But Mridula saw it differently. For her, a home was never about square footage or granite countertops. It was about the lives we built inside it. She worried more about whether the kids had neighbors to play with, safe streets to cycle on, and parks nearby to get dirty in. And after one particularly draining move, she took a quiet promise from me: No more shifting. Not for a long time.

"Let's give the kids roots," she said. "Not just walls."

And she meant it. She worked relentlessly, not just in her own career, but in shaping the world around Niranjan and

Kamakshi. Planning birthday parties, organizing playdates, and managing endless logistics. Even with house help, there were always gaps. And she filled those gaps. Tirelessly. Quietly.

I could comprehend what she meant, and so, I began to change. My decisions slowed down, but sharpened. I said no more easily. Not out of arrogance, but alignment. I stopped chasing scale for its own sake. If a new project didn't excite us culturally, even if it made sense financially, we walked away.

We chose depth over width.

And in that depth, we discovered our real strength: we were building relationships that lasted longer than retainers.

One of the most profound moments during this time wasn't professional. It came at home.

I wasn't always the most hands-on parent. I loved my children deeply, but I wasn't present for the small, formative events. I remember once a friend of Mridula's casually asked me about the upcoming PTM. I paused and said, "What's that?"

Not out of neglect. But out of misalignment. I brought the fun, the lightness, the jokes, and midnight drives. Mridula brought the discipline, the planning, and the nurturing structure that shaped them.

And yet, when the time came, when Niranjan began to step into his own, I slowly took the reins. Never loudly. Never in the foreground. But I began to guide him. Quietly. Firmly. Like I had done with teams all my life: observing, nudging, calibrating. Letting him feel like he had full control, while knowing I was always a step behind, watching, ready.

But that was not the moment. The moment was much deeper than that.

Kamakshi had just learned to walk. She would totter across the room, arms out, eyes big with awe. One night, while I was finishing up on a client call, she tottered towards me, clung to my leg, and smiled up at me with a grin that made all else melt away.

It was such a simple moment. And yet, I remember standing there, laptop still open, and thinking: This is the real ROI.

Not the revenue. Not the reviews.

But this, being here, fully. Not in spirit. In presence.

Mridula, ever the quiet backbone of our lives, just nodded at me from the kitchen. She saw it too. That I had finally come home, not just physically, but emotionally.

My mother, watching all this from her corner seat, said something that evening that I carry with me even now.

“You’ve stopped running. Not because you’re tired, but because you’ve found something worth walking toward.”

I didn’t reply. I just held her hand.

Because she was right.

That’s the part no one tells you about entrepreneurship. It’s not a leap. It’s a return. To who you were before you were told what you should be.

And so I kept building.

We hired slowly. Trained patiently. Listened constantly. We made mistakes, of course. But we owned them. Fixed them. Learned from them.

We didn't call it a "team." We called it a crew. And we ran it like a ship, not in discipline alone, but in spirit. Everyone mattered. Everyone was seen.

By the end of the second year, we were breaking even. Not just financially, but emotionally. The guilt was gone. The fear had faded. And the pressure had turned into presence.

One evening, I sat down with Niranjan for a school project. He was researching different careers. He turned to me and asked, "Papa, what do you do?"

It was such a basic question. But it caught me off guard.

"I build things," I said.

"What kind of things?"

I thought for a second.

"Things that help people do their work better. Things that fix what's broken."

He nodded, satisfied.

And I smiled, because for the first time in years, that answer felt true.

This wasn't just a career move.

It was a correction. A course correction toward alignment, intention, and purpose.

But as with every journey, just when things start to feel steady, the winds begin to shift.

The next phase wouldn't be about launching.

It would be about learning how to hold the wheel when storms arrive.

But that's a story for another time.

For now, I was exactly where I needed to be.

Not at the top. Not in the spotlight.

But at the beginning of something real.

Chapter 4: The First Failures: Where It Almost Ended

Success, when it comes quietly, often carries a warning disguised as a compliment.

"You're doing so well. You should think bigger."

At first, that kind of praise feels like encouragement. A validation of the long nights, the quiet sacrifices, the endless recalibration that it took to build something real. And for a while, I believed it. Not out of arrogance, but out of a desire to keep moving forward. To not become complacent. To grow before we stalled.

By our third year, Aethon was stable. More than stable, it was respected. We had steady clients, referrals flowing in, and a small but committed crew that knew why we existed and what we stood for. We weren't just delivering on contracts. We were building a reputation.

And then, the conversations began.

"Why don't you diversify?"

"You're already solving core problems, why not go upstream?"

"There's money being left on the table."

They weren't wrong. At least, not on paper.

We had relationships with traders. Many of them were exposed to freight volatility. Chartering was a natural adjacency. We understood operations. We could hedge their positions with a dry bulk desk. It made strategic sense.

Around the same time, I was introduced to a property group in the UK. They pitched a real estate venture - small, manageable, with potential for development-led returns. We'd come in with capital and board-level oversight. They'd handle execution. It sounded neat. Controlled. Logical.

And so, we took the plunge.

Not all at once. Carefully. Gradually. We ran models. Held meetings. Structured everything. On paper, we did our due diligence.

But what we didn't account for was something we had long known in theory but had ignored in excitement: paper is clean. Reality is not.

The chartering venture began with confidence. We brought in a few seasoned professionals, set up a light structure, and started talking to clients. At first, it went well. Deals closed. Margins looked healthy. Our name helped open doors. Clients liked the idea of an execution-led operator. We positioned ourselves as more reliable than the usual market cowboys.

But soon, the cracks appeared.

Chartering is a world built on instinct, speed, and unspoken alliances. We were operating with precision, but lacking depth. We trusted people too fast. The partners we had barely tested. Information we hadn't cross-verified. Decisions that felt urgent but weren't truly ours to rush.

One particular deal stands out.

A client wanted a spot fixture - a time-sensitive parcel move. Our commercial partner pushed for a quick commitment.

Rates were moving. Competition was circling. We agreed. The math checked out. The risk was "hedged."

It wasn't.

The vessel underperformed. Demurrage disputes began. The client got squeezed. We absorbed the hit, not just in cash, but in credibility. Emails flew. Calls became terse. The relationship frayed.

That deal became our first public bruise.

The dry bulk desk limped on. We tried to correct. Brought in legal counsel. Reviewed charters more tightly. But the market had moved. Sentiment had changed. And internally, we were beginning to fragment.

The team that handled our core services began feeling peripheral. "Is this who we are now?" someone asked in a team meeting.

I didn't have an answer.

Because in chasing scale, I had momentarily lost sight of soul.

But things didn't stop there. I was keen on correcting things, but I wanted to grow, too. So, I came up with another bold decision, one everyone in the team thought could elevate us further: vessel ownership.

After years of operating and chartering ships, the idea of owning tonnage felt like a natural progression. We were approached with a deal - mid-life vessel, attractively priced, distressed seller. On paper, it looked smart.

But we moved too fast.

We bought the vessel. And within weeks, the operational reality hit us.

Deferred maintenance. Regulatory gaps. Crew issues. Delayed clearances. Charter interest that didn't materialize. What we had framed as an asset quickly became a floating liability - burning cash, eroding confidence.

It wasn't just a bad deal. It was a bad assumption: that just because we understood operations, we were ready for ownership. The gap between managing a vessel and owning one hit us hard.

Every time I saw the ship's name in our internal reports, it reminded me: depth of insight beats breadth of ambition.

At the same time, the UK real estate play was also showing signs of strain.

The property group we had partnered with began missing deadlines. Construction delays. Regulatory issues. Local council approvals that hadn't been factored into the initial timeline. We pushed back. Asked for clarity.

They gave us slide decks.

But the ground reality was different.

Progress was slow. Cost overruns began. And worst of all, communication stopped being transparent. We were getting updates after the fact, not before.

One evening, after a frustrating call with the partners, I remember walking into the living room and collapsing onto the couch. Mridula sat beside me, silent. I didn't say much. Just one sentence: "I trusted the wrong people."

She didn't respond with advice.

She just placed her hand on my shoulder.

That's the thing about failure. When it arrives, it rarely announces itself as a collapse. It arrives as fatigue. As a doubt. As the slow unraveling of things you thought were secure.

We tried to course correct. Pulled back from further investment. Called for audits. Hired a local consultant to give us on-ground intelligence. What we found confirmed our fears.

Oversights. Overpromises. And a complete mismatch between the vision we had bought into and the execution we were now stuck with.

The financial losses weren't catastrophic. But they were significant.

Emotionally, it felt worse.

Because these weren't losses from negligence. They were losses from misjudgment.

From believing we could extend our principles to partners who didn't share them.

From trusting speed over depth.

From assuming that early success gave us clarity in domains we hadn't yet earned the right to play in.

The reputational impact was subtle, but sharp. Word travels fast. Especially in tight-knit industries. We had been the disciplined newcomers who were building something clean. And now, we had entered messier waters. People noticed.

Internally, I could feel the mood shift.

The Aethon team, once tight and aligned, began asking quiet questions. Were we losing focus? Who were we becoming?

And I didn't blame them.

Because I had the same questions.

At night, I'd stare at the whiteboard that once held our core philosophy: "We don't sell services. We deliver trust."

And I'd wonder: Had I broken my own code?

That question stayed with me.

It haunted me not because we had failed. But because we had failed to stay true.

That was harder to forgive.

The thing about early success is that it clouds your instinct. It makes you believe you're seeing clearly when really, you're seeing selectively. Confirmation bias creeps in quietly. You notice only what validates your next step, not what questions it raises.

That's how we walked into both ventures, with intelligence, yes. But also with an assumption.

And when they began to collapse, I didn't feel anger. I felt a slow disillusionment.

I had built Aethon on conviction, on craft, on values that were forged in the trenches of employment and refined in the early years of service. We didn't scale for headlines. We scaled because we had earned the right to. And now, in the name of growth, I had invited chaos into a system that had once felt clean.

That realization came not through a major crisis, but through a small, almost forgettable moment.

One afternoon, our operations head walked into my cabin and dropped a file on my desk.

"Three small accounts have pulled back. Said we're no longer as responsive."

The amount wasn't large. The clients weren't marquee.

But I froze.

Because they were right.

We had stopped being responsive. Not because we didn't care. But because we were distracted. Spread. Disjointed. And in that moment, I saw it all at once, not the financial bleeding, but the cultural drift.

The very DNA of the company was shifting, and I had let it happen.

That evening, I sat alone in the office after everyone had left. No music. No laptop. Just a blank notepad.

And a question.

What have I become too proud to admit?

I wrote that at the top of the page.

Then waited.

Nothing came for ten minutes.

Then, slowly:

- I moved too fast.
- I confused activity with momentum.
- I wanted to prove we could do more before we finished mastering what we had started.
- I trusted people based on pitch, not pattern.
- I said yes too often.

I didn't stop writing until the list reached 19 points.

I folded that paper and slipped it into my wallet.

It's still there.

Because I never want to forget that silence is where most correction begins.

In the weeks that followed, I began to reverse-engineer every decision we had made in those expansions. Not to blame others. But to understand what had shifted in me. Somewhere, I had started chasing identity in ambition. I wanted Aethon to be known not just as excellent, but as expansive. I thought that would give us legitimacy. Validation. Weight.

But in doing so, I forgot a truth I had lived at sea for years: more weight doesn't mean more strength. It just means less stability when the waters change.

And the waters had changed.

My calendar had turned into a battlefield. Meetings about shipping disputes, follow-ups on real estate litigation, and angry investor calls. I wasn't doing the work I loved anymore, I was damage controlling work I didn't even enjoy.

One evening, I sat with Mridula and tried to explain it all. But the words came out jumbled. Frustration, regret, fatigue all blended into one long sentence that didn't land.

She listened quietly. As she always does.

And then, she asked me something that reset everything.

"If this weren't your company, would you still be here?"

I didn't answer.

Because I already knew.

The next morning, I called my core leadership team for a closed-door meeting.

No decks. No reports.

Just the truth.

I laid everything on the table: the losses, the misjudgments, the cultural drift. I admitted every flaw in our decision-making process, every oversight, every ego-driven call.

There was silence at first.

Then one of our senior project leads, someone who had been with me since year one, said, "We've been waiting for this conversation."

Not in defiance. In relief.

Because when leadership pretends, the whole team holds its breath.

We ended that meeting not with strategy, but with understanding.

And over the next three months, we began cleaning up.

We pulled out of the real estate venture. It was expensive, complicated, and ugly. But we did it. Piece by piece. We negotiated settlements. Absorbed losses. Walked away without drama, but with discipline.

In the chartering vertical, we stopped new business completely. Handled the existing contracts with full diligence. Paid where we had to. Wrote off what we couldn't recover. More importantly, we reached out to clients directly, not to spin the story, but to tell them the truth.

Some respected it.

Some left anyway.

Both were fair.

Internally, I made one major change.

I created a principle I called "core priority bias." If something wasn't directly strengthening our core service, culture, or capability, it was delayed, deprioritized, or dropped. No exceptions. Not even mine.

It wasn't just a business reset.

It was a return to self.

I began to speak differently in team reviews. Slower. Softer. Less certainty, more clarity. I didn't pretend to have all the answers. I invited questions more openly. Encouraged people to challenge, to spot drift before it deepened.

One day, during a team training session, a young associate stood up and asked, "What's the biggest thing you've learned from this failure?"

I paused. Thought about it.

And said, "That losing money is hard. But losing your reflection in the mirror is worse."

That line stayed with the team. I saw it pop up in Slack threads, in whiteboard corners, even in someone's email signature months later.

Because they felt it too.

The beauty of early failure is that it's not fatal. It doesn't end you. But it tests everything you say you believe. And if you survive it, you become less decorative and more durable.

That's what began to happen at Aethon.

We became quieter.

But stronger.

Our client list shrank. Our revenue dipped. But our conviction returned.

And so did my energy.

Not all at once.

But in steady, human doses.

Not all lessons are loud. Some arrive slowly, like a tide on sand, carving new lines, erasing old ones, and leaving behind only what's meant to stay.

When I look back on those years now, the slip into chaos, the long correction, the slow return, I don't see failure in the way the world defines it. I see mirrors. I see echoes. I see the difference between what is built for applause and what is built for resilience.

There's a kind of courage no one prepares you for, the courage it takes to stay when things are not working, to not cut and run, to fix what you broke with your own hands.

That's the courage I had to find.

Because walking away from a failed venture is easy. Owning it, cleaning it, absorbing the shockwaves, not just professionally, but personally, that's the part that tests your spine.

The real cost of those failures wasn't financial. Yes, we lost money. But we made it back. What lingered longer was something deeper, the self-doubt that creeps in when your instinct misfires. The guilt of dragging your team into storms they didn't choose. The humiliation, not of public criticism, but of watching something you believed in unravel because you didn't listen soon enough.

I had to forgive myself for that.

Not quickly. Not conveniently. But honestly.

I remember one weekend retreat I attended during that period. It wasn't a leadership conference. Just a quiet gathering of professionals from different walks of life, founders, teachers, architects, and civil servants. One of the sessions asked us to share a story we had never spoken aloud before. Not a pitch. Not a highlight reel. Just a story that still held weight.

When my turn came, I spoke about the real estate venture.

Not the numbers. The feeling.

The feeling of walking into a site in London and realizing the paperwork had missed key compliance documentation. The feeling of calling the local partner and getting voicemail for three straight days. The feeling of facing the team back home and saying, "This one's on me."

I told them how that weight stayed with me.

How I had built a company on precision, and then lost my own coordinates.

When I finished, no one clapped. That wasn't the point. But a woman sitting across the circle, a former NGO head, said softly, "Sometimes the scar is the certificate."

That sentence stayed with me.

Because that's what those years became.

Not a chapter to hide.

But a certificate I earned.

Proof that I could navigate failure not by pretending it didn't happen, but by letting it change me.

Change the way I decide.

Change the way I delegate.

Change the way I define success.

And slowly, almost invisibly, that change began to reflect in how I led.

I became slower to commit.

Not because I doubted everything, but because I had learned the cost of premature certainty.

I asked more questions in meetings, not to interrogate, but to calibrate.

When a team member pitched a bold idea, I no longer asked, "What's the upside?"

I asked, "What happens if it doesn't work?"

Not to discourage them. But to prepare them.

Because I had learned that readiness isn't about being sure.

It's about knowing what you'll do when the answer is no.

And that shift, subtle, persistent, quiet, began to ripple outward.

Our decision-making got cleaner.

Our internal debates got healthier.

And our culture got deeper.

Because nothing bonds a team more than surviving a storm together, and choosing to stay.

One of the proudest moments for me came not during a product launch or a client win, but during an internal farewell.

A project manager, one of our earliest team members, was relocating abroad. On his last day, the team organized a small send-off. Speeches, laughter, and snacks. I said a few words, mostly gratitude.

But before leaving, he handed me a note. Just a folded slip of paper.

It said, *"You didn't protect us from failure. You led us through it. That's why I'll always carry this place with me."*

I didn't respond. I just nodded.

Because that's the kind of legacy I wanted.

Not perfection.

Presence.

And that presence extended beyond the walls of work.

At home, I was also shifting.

I stopped bringing stress to the dinner table. Not because I had resolved everything, but because I had learned how to contain it.

I began playing with Niranjan again without glancing at my phone. Started reading bedtime stories to Kamakshi with full attention, not just voice, but heart.

Mridula noticed the difference.

"You're here," she said once.

And I knew exactly what she meant.

Because during those chaotic months of ambition and anxiety, I had become a ghost in my own home. Physically present, emotionally distant.

But now, I was returning.

Not as a victor.

As a witness.

To what mattered.

And that witnessing became my new compass.

In every meeting, every decision, every pitch, I began to ask myself one quiet question:

Does this take me closer to who I want to become?

If the answer wasn't a full yes, I paused.

Not because I had become cautious, but because I had become clear.

And clarity, I learned, isn't about having fewer options. It's about having stronger boundaries.

That's what the failures taught me. That the goal of leadership isn't expansion. It's alignment. And alignment is not achieved in times of ease. It's carved during the crises, when your values are tested, your choices are exposed, and your people are watching to see if your words hold up under weight.

Ours did.

Eventually.

But only because we chose to stay with the mess. Not edit it. Not run from it.

Stay with it.

And in that staying, we discovered our spine.

That's what I carry with me now.

Not a roadmap.

A rhythm.

And that rhythm says: grow slow. Listen deep. Speak less. Mean more.

It's not glamorous.

But it's real.

And real, I've learned, always survives the storm.

Chapter 5: The Karma Rebirth - When Dubai Met Destiny

Some changes arrive like storms, loud, sweeping, impossible to ignore. Others arrive like whispers. Subtle. Internal. You only notice them when something you used to chase no longer pulls at you.

After the clean-up, after the course correction, after the quiet rebuilding of Aethon, I should've felt satisfied. We had made it through the fire. We had come out clearer, leaner, stronger. But I didn't feel victorious. I felt still. Deeply still. And in that stillness, something inside me shifted again.

I realized I didn't just want to recover.

I wanted to reimagine.

There's a peculiar discomfort that sets in when what once felt like a destination begins to feel like a hallway. You're not lost. But you know you can't stay. That's how I felt, sitting in Aethon's boardroom one morning, reviewing a perfectly solid report, listening to perfectly smart people say perfectly accurate things. And yet, a quiet voice inside me asked, Is this still yours?

That voice wouldn't go away.

It didn't shout. It simply lingered.

And so, I turned east.

To Dubai.

Dubai had always intrigued me. Not just for its wealth or skyline, but for its energy. There's a rhythm to this city, a kind of unapologetic ambition paired with a rare openness. It's a city that doesn't wait for permission. It builds. Fast. Bold. But not without feeling.

We weren't strangers to it. We had already been active there since 2010, working under the Centurion banner. Steady real estate investments, sensible development plays, nothing flashy, but rooted. That foundation gave us access. But this new shift wasn't about access. It was about awakening.

I didn't want to expand.

I wanted to create again.

And the first spark didn't strike in Dubai at all.

It struck in Cyprus.

It's strange how sometimes you have to step into entirely new soil to remember who you are. Cyprus felt different. Calmer. The light softer. The pace slower. But the possibility, wide open. We weren't chasing margins there. We were building homes, real ones. Villas with light that streamed in just right. Kitchens that felt like they could hold long conversations. Spaces that weren't about grandeur, but about grounding.

That's where Karma was born.

Not as a brand.

As a feeling.

We didn't market it heavily. We didn't throw big numbers around. But people came. They walked into those spaces and felt something they hadn't felt in a long time: ease.

And just like that, Karma wasn't just a project.

It was a philosophy.

One that began to shape more than floor plans. It began to shape me.

My Cypriot citizenship followed, not as a strategy, but as a kind of affirmation. Karma had given me more than a business. It had given me belonging. A sense of rootedness in a place where no one expected anything from me, except authenticity.

That sense of clarity followed me back to Dubai.

And this time, when I looked at the city, I didn't see competition or chaos.

I saw a canvas.

We didn't launch Karma in Dubai with fireworks. We arrived quietly. Elegantly. Every deal was deliberate. Every project carried an energy map as much as an engineering plan. We bought off-market. We upgraded with care. We placed mirrors not just for aesthetic, but for energy flow. We named homes after values. Synced purchases with planetary movements. Not to be trendy. But to be truthful, to whom I had become.

COVID came shortly after.

For most of the world, it was a standstill.

For us, it was a portal.

Dubai stayed open when others shut down. Moved when others froze. And in that rare window of pause, we found an unexpected surge.

While others were holding back, we were stepping in.

We bought properties that no one else was looking at. Vessels that were deemed "sinking ships." Businesses that had potential buried under panic. Everyone saw risk. We saw reset.

And strangely, beautifully, those moves paid off.

Not just in numbers.

But in alignment.

There was one project in particular that no one wanted. An underdeveloped block, stuck in legal knots, halfway to becoming a write-off. I remember walking the site alone one late afternoon. Dust swirling. Scaffolding rusting. But I could see the final layout in my mind. I could feel where the main entrance would breathe better if shifted ten feet. I could hear the silence that would fill the courtyard if the proportions were respected.

We bought it.

Reworked every detail.

Two years later, it became one of our most elegant transformations.

Not a skyscraper.

A sanctuary.

That's what Karma became known for.

Not size.

But soul.

What I began to understand, slowly and then all at once, was that real estate isn't just about structures.

It's about states.

States of mind. States of being. States of alignment.

Somewhere along the way, Karma stopped being a business. It became a ritual. A way of building that didn't begin with a blueprint, it began with a question: How will this place make someone feel?

That question guided everything.

The angle of a balcony. The scent of the wood. The way the light hit the wall at 4:15 p.m. These weren't details anymore. They were decisions.

Because when someone walks into a home, they aren't buying brick and marble. They're buying the possibility of peace. The imagination of a new rhythm. And if you pay close enough attention, you realize, real estate can either drain or restore.

We chose restoration.

There was a villa we were renovating, nothing extravagant, but it had potential. The original plan called for maximizing built-up area. Bigger rooms, more fittings, modern textures.

I scrapped it.

Not out of rebellion, but respect. The house wanted space. It needed silence. We trimmed walls, moved a staircase, and shifted a window just to frame a single tree outside. The architect was baffled. "You're reducing revenue."

I nodded. "But we're increasing reverence."

When it was done, the buyers didn't ask about square footage. They stood in the living room, watched the light pour in, and said, "It feels right."

That became our design metric.

Does it feel right?

In time, Karma began attracting clients who didn't want marketing brochures. They wanted meaning. They didn't ask about ROI. They asked about energy. They didn't want to be sold to. They wanted to be understood.

And for the first time in years, I was doing work that felt less like solving and more like serving.

Meanwhile, something beautiful was taking shape beside me.

Mridula.

She had always been the quiet pulse in our lives. Steady, graceful, never seeking credit, but always adding something invisible and invaluable. But now, she was stepping into her own orbit. And the world was beginning to notice.

It started simply, with décor suggestions for a Karma villa. Then a full interiors project. Then a client who said, "Who did this? I want her to do my next one."

And slowly, ZENA was born.

Not as an extension of Karma.

But as her own energy field.

Where Karma built the space, ZENA refined the soul of it.

Mridula didn't speak in budgets or timelines. She spoke in moods. In hues. In feelings that lingered after the furniture was set.

She had an eye I didn't. Where I saw alignment, she saw softness. Where I saw function, she saw flow. And watching her work was like watching grace unfold in architecture.

We never sat down and decided to "build together." It happened on its own. Like vines finding each other in a garden. Some evenings, we'd sit side by side after the kids were asleep, sketching layouts, arguing over textures, measuring silence between our suggestions.

There was no competition. Just co-creation.

Sometimes she'd reject one of my layout ideas with a simple, "Too masculine."

Other times, I'd ask her to add just a hint more structure. "It needs grounding," I'd say.

And in between those notes, a partnership began to bloom, one not based on title or transaction, but on trust.

ZENA grew fast. Not because it was marketed well, but because it was felt. People walked into those spaces and saw her signature, even if they couldn't name it.

Clients began requesting "the Mridula touch."

And I watched, quietly proud, as she navigated her projects with elegance and quiet command.

She wasn't copying Karma.

She was complimenting it.

Where I dealt in blueprints, she dealt in blue light.

And somewhere between our two rhythms, something new began to take shape.

A shared vocabulary.

We didn't call it a strategy. It was more intuitive than that.

We'd drive through neighborhoods not looking for land, but for potential.

I'd point to a corner plot and say, "Too much chaos on that street."

She'd nod, "You felt that too?"

I'd suggest a buyer for a development. She'd pause and say, "Not this one. The energy doesn't match."

We were designing karma.

Together.

Not in the karmic debt kind of way.

But in the intentionality sense.

We believed, deeply, that what you build reflects what you carry. And if you build from fear, it shows. If you build from ego, it shows. But if you build from stillness, from service, from beauty, from care, that, too, shows.

So we built from stillness.

And Dubai, to our quiet surprise, responded.

People began to speak of Karma not as a company, but as a space you enter. Something you feel before you buy. A name that whispered, not shouted.

We weren't trying to disrupt the market.

We were trying to dignify it.

No billboards. No media splashes. No vanity awards.

Just consistency. Elegance. Precision.

Even our vendor meetings changed. We started asking our suppliers about their own well-being. Not as small talk, but as part of the process. If they weren't aligned, the project suffered. So we aligned the people first.

One of our electricians, brilliant but erratic, once showed up late for a site review. When I asked why, he confessed that he was juggling too many side jobs. I told him, gently but clearly, "We're not just paying for your hands. We're trusting your energy."

He teared up.

"Sir, no one's ever said that to me before."

That's when I realized: we weren't just building homes.

We were shifting lives.

At some point, Karma stopped being a company and became a compass.

It wasn't deliberate. There was no branding exercise. No mission statement workshop. It just happened, like breath returning after a long swim. I stopped thinking in metrics and began thinking in moments. In meaning. In memory.

And that changed everything.

We began to time our launches not by market cycles, but by alignment, astrological, emotional, and even energetic. Some called it superstition. I called it intuition. Because it wasn't about predicting success. It was about honoring flow.

I had started reading more deeply into Vedic astrology during this period. Not to become an expert. Just to understand patterns. Movement. Cosmic geometry that had been respected for thousands of years.

I found something strangely familiar in it.

Shipping had taught me to read wind direction. Business had taught me to read risk. But astrology taught me to read resonance.

I started scheduling internal launches during auspicious windows. Not because I thought it guaranteed success, but because it reminded us that timing isn't just a spreadsheet concept. It's spiritual, too.

Even our property numbers were carefully selected. Not for vanity. For vibration. I remember one client asking, "You really changed the door number just for a sense of alignment?"

I nodded.

"It's not just a door. It's the energy that walks through it."

These weren't gimmicks.

They were signals, to ourselves, to our teams, to the universe, that we were paying attention. That we were building with more than concrete. We were building with consciousness.

We named our villas after virtues: Sattva, Artha, and Shanti. We designed corners to invite stillness. Entryways to carry welcome. And none of this was written in the sales brochures. It didn't need to be.

Because people felt it.

A family once visited a site on a quiet Tuesday morning. They were from Europe, not particularly spiritual. As they walked through the hallway, the wife paused and said, “There’s a peace here I can’t explain.”

That was our confirmation.

We didn’t need pitch decks.

We needed presence.

And the more we honored that, the more the city responded. Karma began attracting a different kind of clientele, not transactional, but intentional. Artists. Thinkers. Philanthropists. Families going through transitions, divorces, retirements, and fresh starts.

They didn’t just want homes.

They wanted healing.

And we became the quiet conduit.

It wasn’t just Dubai anymore. Karma was reaching out across continents. A family from Cyprus brought friends from South Africa. A businessman from Singapore visited a villa and said, “This is the first property I’ve walked into that felt like it had a soul.”

I remember sitting in that very living room after he left. Mridula was adjusting a curtain detail, not for symmetry, but for softness.

She looked at me and smiled. “They feel it because we do.”

That’s when I realized we were no longer in real estate.

We were in remembrance.

Helping people remember how spaces could feel.

How homes could hold you.

How architecture could become a kind of assurance.

And that shift, subtle, spiritual, silent, began to transform the way I led.

I no longer chased markets. I listened to them.

I didn't argue with the timing. I aligned with it.

I didn't try to control growth. I curated it.

That doesn't mean we stopped being strategic.

It means we became more selective, with projects, with people, with partners.

I started turning down opportunities more often. Not out of ego. Out of awareness.

If a deal didn't feel right, if the energy in the first meeting was off, if the intention behind it smelled of hurry or hunger, I stepped back.

Even when the numbers looked good.

Especially when they looked too good.

That discipline, rare in a city built on speed, became our secret edge.

We weren't first. We were right.

And that gave us longevity.

One afternoon, over tea, a veteran developer asked me, "How do you manage to stay off the radar and still close such meaningful work?"

I answered without thinking. "I don't try to stay off the radar. I just try to stay in rhythm."

He laughed.

But I meant it.

Because I had learned that most chaos comes from forcing what isn't ready. And most clarity comes from waiting with presence.

And that patience - it wasn't easy. But it was sacred.

It meant fewer projects.

But deeper ones.

Fewer clients.

But clearer alignment.

And slowly, Karma became less about output and more about offering.

That awareness began to ripple through the team.

We started onboarding people differently.

Our interviews began with a question: "What are you building in your own life?"

If the answer had depth, even if it wasn't polished, we explored further.

Because we weren't just hiring skills.

We were welcoming frequency.

And frequency doesn't lie.

We turned down candidates with impeccable experience, but heavy energy.

We welcomed younger professionals who walked into the room with curiosity, clarity, and kindness.

And every time we trusted that compass, it paid off.

Not always instantly.

But inevitably.

Because when your team carries intention, your work carries integrity.

And when your work carries integrity, your brand doesn't need to shout.

It hums.

That's what Karma became.

A hum in the city.

Not loud.

But unmistakable.

Every builder has a blueprint.

Some follow one drawn by convention. Some follow one dictated by markets. But a few follow something quieter. A blueprint etched not in lines and layouts, but in lessons. And if you've listened long enough to your own life, you begin to realize: your path was never random.

It was designed.

Not on paper. But in a pattern.

That's how Karma began to feel. Less like a venture. More like a return. To a rhythm that had always been with me, even at sea. Even in boardrooms. Even in those chaotic early years of entrepreneurship.

It had just been waiting for me to slow down enough to hear it.

When I did, the entire game changed.

We weren't building for projections anymore. We were building for presence.

We didn't ask, "How many units?" We asked, "How does this space hold stillness?"

We didn't aim to impress. We aimed to resonate.

And in that quiet recalibration, I began to redefine what legacy meant.

Legacy, I used to think, was what you left behind.

Now, I understood: it's what you live into.

It's not the name on the building. It's the feeling inside the walls. It's not the plaque. It's the peace. It's not the story others tell about you. It's the story people tell themselves when they enter something you've created.

I saw that in Karma's clients.

One family, originally from Lebanon, walked through one of our properties and paused at the doorway. The father turned to his teenage daughter and said, "We don't have to keep searching. This one listens."

I remember that word.

Listens.

Not looks good.

Not feels big.

Listens.

That's what real spaces do.

And that's what real leadership does, too.

It listens.

That became the way I led, not from the front, not from the top, but from the inside.

I began spending less time on pitches and more time on presence.

Less time on strategy and more time on silence.

I'd visit sites early in the morning, before anyone arrived. Walk the space. No clipboard. No checklist. Just breath. Just listening.

Sometimes I'd feel something was off, a hallway too narrow, a view too blocked, a tone too sharp. I didn't always know the fix. But the space told me something wasn't right.

And when we corrected it, you could feel the difference.

That's when I stopped saying we were in real estate altogether.

We were in resonance.

Helping people return to themselves through space.

Helping teams find alignment through intention.

Helping families feel safe, not just structurally, but spiritually.

And as this clarity deepened, so did my sense of calm.

I stopped checking numbers every day. Not because they didn't matter. But because they weren't driving me anymore.

They were following me. Following the frequency we had chosen. The consistency we had embodied.

One evening, Mridula and I sat on the rooftop of one of our completed projects. The sun had just set. Lights from the city flickered on slowly, like stars remembering their place. She looked out over the skyline and said, “Do you realize we’ve built a rhythm that doesn’t burn us out?”

I nodded.

Because that was the deepest truth of all.

We weren’t building to escape.

We weren’t building to compete.

We were building to remember.

To remember what mattered. To remember how peace feels. To remember what it means to create without depletion.

And that remembrance became the heart of everything.

Even our children felt it.

Niranjan, now older, would ask questions about layout balance and energy flow. Kamakshi would walk into a new site and say, “This one feels grumpy,” with total sincerity.

We didn’t correct them.

We learned from them.

Because they were closer to the essence than most adults in suits.

And in many ways, Karma wasn’t just our creation.

It was our family’s unfolding.

A map of our becoming.

Mridula's ZENA had become a quiet force of its own. Her spaces carried grace. Her teams operated with harmony. She didn't raise her voice in meetings. She didn't sell herself. She just delivered beauty with such integrity that the world leaned in.

I once asked her, "What's your metric for success?"

She smiled. "When a client says nothing. Just stands in the room and breathes."

That answer changed how I approached everything.

We stopped overexplaining. Stopped chasing approval. We let our work speak. And it did. In wood, in light, in stillness.

Dubai, in return, gave us space. It allowed us to build without noise. To grow without compromise. To create without erasure.

And that's what destiny really is.

Not fate.

But frequency.

When who you are, what you do, and where you are align.

That's what happened in Dubai.

We didn't just meet a market.

We met ourselves.

Not the selves we had to be in the early hustle. Not the selves we were when cleaning up failure. But the selves we were always becoming.

And that's why I call it rebirth.

Not a reinvention.

A rebirth.

Because everything I was, captain, operator, founder, father, came together here.

Not in a role.

In a rhythm.

From ship deck to skyline, the transition wasn't about scale. It was about the soul. About taking the same discipline, the same presence, the same belief in order, and applying it to something quieter, but just as vast.

And Karma became the container.

Not of profit.

Of purpose.

Of remembering that what we build will outlive us. And how we build will echo longer than any brochure or balance sheet.

That's what this chapter of life became.

A return.

To the truth.

To trust.

To karma.

Chapter 6: Expanding the Vision - Real Estate, Shipping & More

The danger of success is that it often whispers to you, "Now you can rest." But if you've built your life on storms and second winds, you know better.

For me, expansion never came with fanfare. It came quietly. Like a tide pulling back, exposing the rocks beneath the surface. The world saw Karma Developers taking root in Dubai, saw elegance and curation. But what they didn't see was the storm just behind my smile, the kind of inner urgency that builds not from greed, but from gravity.

The year was 2020. The world was recovering from its collective exhale, that strange silence the pandemic had carved across borders and balance sheets. Some called it a reset. I called it a revelation.

I had spent years refining, rebalancing, and reimagining. From 2019 to 2022, I worked on multiple fronts, from bringing business back into my own hands to restructuring multiple other businesses, keeping what was needed and letting go of what wasn't required.

Karma was no longer just a brand. It had evolved into a belief system. A way of building that didn't sacrifice soul for scale. But I could feel something shifting. Not in the markets, but within me.

I wasn't looking to expand because I was hungry. I was looking to expand because I was ready.

That distinction matters.

Hunger can blur vision. Readiness clarifies it.

So, I began again.

This time, it wasn't just Karma. It was real estate in new geographies. Shipping in new forms. Education. Capital. And at the heart of it all, the one business that never left my side, Aethon.

Aethon Marine Services had always been my lifeline. Even when it stood quietly in the background, behind the glow of Karma's architectural brilliance, it was always there, like the sea beneath the ship, invisible to most but vital to movement. We continued acquiring ships, operating with precision, and executing financial maneuvers that would sound insane to anyone not seasoned in the calculus of maritime risk.

To outsiders, it seemed I had become a real estate magnate.

To me, I was still a captain.

Only now, I was steering more than vessels.

We moved into the UK market, tentatively at first. The sophistication was high, but so was the resistance. Regulations were dense, and the margin for error was cruel. But we adapted, as we always had. We studied. We hired the right voices. We failed forward. And most importantly, we respected the market's personality before trying to shape it.

Romania was different. It was raw. Honest. Still forming its identity in many ways. But there's something about building where others hesitate; it makes you sharper, more alive. We found joy there in the simplicity of transactions, in the possibility that hadn't yet been colonized by consultants and middlemen.

Cyprus remained close to my heart. It wasn't just where Karma had found early soil; it was where I had found my second passport. The sense of belonging. The reminder that sometimes, geography gifts you more than land; it gives you a new lens on life.

And of course, Dubai remained the anchor. In this city, I found the freedom to build as boldly as I dared. Off-market properties. Land deals that most wouldn't touch without three levels of approvals. But I didn't wait for green lights. I looked for open windows.

Because the ones who expand with confidence aren't the ones who control everything, they're the ones who can move before the room realizes there's a shift.

That's what 2020 taught me.

We didn't just expand. We erupted.

Across continents. Across verticals. Across assumptions.

People asked me often, "What's the secret?" I'd tell them the truth: There isn't one. Unless you count experience carved from fire, and a team willing to bleed alongside you.

But not every move was golden.

Some of the hardest losses came not in shipping or land, but in people. I had trusted too easily. Backed ventures based on personalities, not performance. Given capital to charisma. Extended equity based on potential, not proof.

It was noble, perhaps. But naive.

I learned that some of the most expensive lines on a balance sheet aren't monetary. They're emotional.

Because when you trust and it fails, it doesn't just cost you returns. It costs you reflection.

I had to sit with those mistakes. Let them teach me what instinct hadn't warned.

Not everyone who walks with you is walking toward the same destination.

Some are walking with mirrors.

Others with masks.

And it took a few brutal lessons to learn that visibility is not a luxury. It's a necessity.

By 2023, I took the reins back.

Not out of anger. Out of clarity.

We began restructuring. Projects were audited. Partnerships revisited. If there was no shared stake in the risk, we exited. If there was opacity, we opted out.

I no longer funded dreams I didn't co-author.

We redrew the map.

One team. One thread. One ethos.

Karma Developers became the flagship again, but now it carried the strength of a failure-clarified vision. We built not just villas and towers, but also intention. Every development bore our fingerprint. Every material chosen with care. Every project pulsed with the question: Does this space heal, or does it just sell?

We branched into tech education through Spectrum Networks. Structured, scalable, sovereign. Not a passion project, an ecosystem. We didn't want to create noise. We wanted to create competence. An institution that elevated enterprise readiness, that trained minds not just in tools, but in temperament.

ZENA became more than Mridula's design dream; it became a design doctrine. Where elegance didn't scream, it whispered. Where form followed feeling. I'd watch her review color palettes like a conductor, each shade tuned to human emotion. I used to build with spreadsheets. She built with stillness.

Then there was Silkleaf Capital. Our family office. A different animal entirely. Sharp, focused, surgical. Here, we weren't builders, we were architects of trust. Every investment was weighed not just by return, but by reputation. Every decision filtered through two metrics: alignment and longevity.

And Aethon, it kept sailing.

Still our stealth force. Still our strategic lever.

Sometimes, I'd sit in boardrooms where Karma's name opened doors. And when someone mentioned shipping dismissively, I'd smile. Because what they didn't realize was that Aethon was still our biggest chess piece.

The real power, after all, doesn't always wear a suit. Sometimes it wears silence.

There comes a point in every builder's journey where the question changes.

It's no longer: Can I grow?

It becomes: Should I?

I had grown. That was clear. From boardrooms to ballast tanks, from chartering offices to construction zones, the growth was real. Tangible. But what began to matter more than the number of businesses or buildings was the substance underneath it all.

Were we expanding our capacity, or just our complexity?

That question haunted me.

Because in the world of empire-building, complexity can seduce you. It looks like momentum. It looks like sophistication. But often, it's just noise.

Complexity hides inefficiencies. It breeds silos. It clouds culture. And worst of all, it feeds egos.

I had to confront that within myself.

There were moments I mistook busy for bold. Mistook stacked calendars for significance. Mistook growth charts for fulfillment.

But when the pandemic slowed the world down, I began seeing what I had refused to acknowledge: not every part of the empire was necessary.

Some were legacy lines kept alive by nostalgia. Others were vanity extensions, initiatives that looked impressive on investor decks but drained the team's energy in silence. And a few, frankly, had become distractions. They diluted focus. Dispersed leadership. Distorted our values.

So I did what few in my position are willing to do.

I began cutting.

Not recklessly. Not reactively. But ruthlessly aligned with who we had become.

We asked: Does this serve the vision or just the vanity?

If it didn't serve the vision, it had to go.

There were business units I had personally nurtured. The teams I had handpicked. But alignment had to win over attachment.

We let go of projects where we lacked direct control.

We exited ventures where clarity had been replaced by complication.

We paused investments that didn't match our frequency, not financially, but philosophically.

And what remained?

The real bones of the operation.

The verticals that weren't just profitable, but purposeful.

Karma Developers stood tall, not as a real estate firm, but as an ideology. It had evolved into our expression of what space should mean. We weren't developers. We were storytellers in stone. Creating homes that healed. Communities that inspired. Places that didn't just house people, but held them.

Shipping, through Aethon, remained our hidden engine. Always tactical. Always quiet. But now, more integrated than ever. We acquired vessels with sharper eyes. Reflagged with better foresight. Negotiated charter parties with the kind of calm that only comes from experience forged in failure.

Then came Spectrum Networks.

I had always believed in education, not the kind that fills heads, but the kind that rewires mindsets. Spectrum wasn't built for scale. It was built for sovereignty. For creating leaders who could think, act, and adapt in real time.

ZENA kept blossoming under Mridula's gentle but precise vision. She wasn't just decorating homes; she was designing emotions. ZENA homes didn't follow trends. They followed truths about how light calms the nervous system, how material textures shape behavior, and how layout impacts dialogue.

And finally, Silkleaf Capital.

Our family office became more than a vehicle for wealth management. It became a laboratory for conviction. We didn't just fund ideas, we filtered futures. We studied trends not for profit, but for pattern. What's emerging? What's decaying? What deserves protection?

Each of these verticals survived the fire of inquiry.

They weren't built for scale.

They were built for the soul.

And that's what allowed them to scale, paradoxically, but powerfully.

You see, we had learned a hard truth: Scale built on stress breaks.

But scale built on soul bends and grows.

So, we leaned into the architecture of boldness, not the recklessness of expansion, but the precision of purpose. We weren't just asking, "Can this make money?" We were asking, "Can this carry meaning?"

That's why every new venture, every project, every pitch, was filtered through three questions:

1. Does it align with who we are becoming?
2. Can it operate without draining our integrity?
3. Will it deepen our capacity, not just expand our surface?

These questions became our compass.

And they saved us from ourselves.

Because temptation didn't go away.

Even as we realigned, the world kept presenting new opportunities, new geographies, emerging industries, and moonshot tech.

But I had changed.

Earlier in my journey, I might have jumped. Now, I studied.

I would listen longer than anyone else in the room.

I'd observe who interrupted whom. Who avoided specifics. Who overused jargon.

I'd walk out of meetings with nothing committed, only a feeling.

And I'd sit with that feeling. Until it either sharpened or softened.

Only then would I decide.

Because decision-making is no longer a moment. It's a method. And instinct, I've learned, is just wisdom made quiet.

This slow clarity became our edge.

When others raced, we reflected.

When others scaled recklessly, we scaled with rhythm.

And slowly, a different kind of empire emerged.

Not loud.

Not bloated.

Not scattered.

But surgical. Spiritual. Sharp.

And yet, none of this meant we stopped evolving.

In fact, the clarity gave us more confidence to evolve.

I remember one particular meeting in early 2023. We had just walked away from a promising hospitality project. The numbers looked good. The team was decent. But something felt off, too much rush, too little root.

After the meeting, one of my senior team members said, “Sometimes I think we’re leaving too much on the table.”

I paused, smiled, and replied, “We’re not leaving money on the table. We’re leaving misalignment.”

That line became a filter for everything.

We don’t chase profit.

We protect peace.

We don’t seek growth.

We steward grace.

Because if you build an empire at the cost of your inner stillness, you’re just constructing prisons with prettier paint.

And I refused to live in a golden cage.

So we kept expanding, but only where the terrain matched our truth.

In shipping, we deepened rather than widened. We focused on fewer routes, but higher leverage. In real estate, we moved into high-trust micro-developments, niche, customized, and deeply relational. In education, we launched executive formats, short bursts with deep impact. And in capital, we bet only on founders we would trust with our children, not just our cheques.

And slowly, people began to notice.

Not because we shouted.

But because we showed up consistently, with presence.

Empires, when they crumble, rarely collapse from the outside.

They erode from within, when clarity gives way to comfort, when systems get bloated with shortcuts, and when trust is given too freely without the guardrails of discernment.

I learned this lesson not in the headlines, but in the margins.

The betrayals didn't come as a single storm. They arrived like silent leaks, small breaches of trust, overlooked red flags, unchecked assumptions. And slowly, they cost more than miscalculations ever did.

In my earlier days, I believed in people almost too quickly. I saw ambition as sincerity. Passion as competence. I extended capital based on vision boards and confident pitches, mistaking volume for depth.

But experience sharpened my filters.

I no longer looked at what someone said in a boardroom. I watched what they didn't say after the meeting.

I noticed how people treated those who couldn't benefit them. How they followed up, not just when chasing opportunity, but when handling adversity.

And in those silences, I began to truly see.

Because leadership, I've realized, isn't just about building the right things, it's about choosing the right people to build them with.

I had to unlearn parts of myself. The idealism. The savior instinct. The belief that with the right guidance, anyone could rise.

Not everyone is ready to rise.

And even fewer are ready to rise with you.

So, we rebuilt not just our businesses, but our hiring DNA.

We began choosing slowness over sparkle. Background checks became deeper. Alignment discussions became more philosophical. We didn't just ask about experience, we asked about failure. How someone talks about what broke often tells you more than their highlight reel.

Culture stopped being a buzzword. It became our blueprint.

And it flowed through every company.

At Karma, we moved from traditional org charts to pods, small, self-led teams accountable not just for delivery, but for decision-making. We embedded astrologers alongside architects, not for superstition, but for synchronicity. Energy mattered. Not in a mystical way, but in a practical one.

Projects where timelines constantly slipped, where teams clashed, where materials kept arriving damaged, we began to ask: What's off beneath the surface?

Often, it wasn't a technical issue. It was energetic misalignment.

So, we corrected that. Quietly, intentionally.

In shipping, we became leaner. Fewer partners. Fewer intermediaries. More direct relationships with vessel owners, ports, and charterers. We didn't need more noise; we needed more clarity.

And that clarity flowed into our operations.

Even the design of our new offices changed.

No longer tall glass towers meant to intimidate. But open spaces meant to invite. We placed communal seating next to strategy boards. We eliminated corner offices. Leaders sat among teams. Everyone saw everything.

Transparency didn't just live in our reports; it lived in our architecture.

That changed how people behaved.

Egos melted. Silos softened. Conversations deepened.

The air felt different.

But more than systems, it was the leadership posture that shifted.

I stopped being the answer man.

I became the question man.

Instead of telling teams what to do, I began asking: What are we solving for? What's the real constraint here? Who's feeling the pressure, and who isn't speaking up?

This wasn't management. This was mentoring in motion.

And it built something far stronger than performance.

It built presence.

That's when the results began compounding.

One shipping deal, executed quietly, yielded returns most would assume came from venture tech. One real estate development, rooted in spiritual design, sold out without a single advertisement. One education cohort, curated for quality, led to three new companies being born from its graduates.

This wasn't magic. It was a method.

A method born of clarity, compassion, and compounding trust.

But even as things grew, I remained vigilant.

Because scale is seductive.

It wants you to believe that more equals better.

That larger teams, larger offices, and larger headlines mean success.

But I knew better.

I had seen businesses implode under their own weight. Leaders who became parodies of themselves, disconnected, distracted, and drowning in decisions.

I didn't want that.

So I created a ritual of pause.

Every quarter, no matter how busy, I'd retreat.

No boardrooms. No calls. Just silence.

Sometimes in the mountains. Sometimes by the sea. Sometimes just in my study, phone off, incense lit, and a blank diary open.

And I would ask myself:

Am I expanding to impress, or to express?

Is this the path of alignment or achievement?

What needs pruning, not promoting?

Those retreats saved me.

From burnout. From blindness. From the illusion of invincibility.

And in those spaces, I began reconnecting with something deeper.

A sense that my work wasn't just economic, it was energetic.

Every decision, every hire, every negotiation was leaving a mark. Not just on balance sheets, but on lives.

That realization made me slower.

Not sluggish.

Just more sacred.

I began writing more. Not for the world. For myself. Reflections on leadership. Notes to my children. Letters I may never send.

And in those writings, a new chapter began forming, not of business, but of legacy.

I started asking: What am I leaving behind?

Not in assets.

But in atmospheres.

When someone walks into a Karma property twenty years from now, will they feel peace?

When a former Spectrum student leads a company, will they lead with grace?

When my team looks back at their time here, will they remember pressure or presence?

That's when I knew: expansion wasn't about more.

It was about meaning.

We weren't building to exit.

We were building to echo.

And echoes don't come from volume.

They come from the depths.

Expansion doesn't always look like growth. Sometimes it looks like quiet.

Not silence, but quiet, of the mind, of decisions, of the inner knowing that you no longer have to prove anything.

I remember a morning in Dubai, early 2024. Karma had just acquired a rare corner plot in one of the city's most contested zones. Off-market. No brokers. Just trust. Just timing.

The deal had taken months. Not because it was complex, but because it had to be right. Everything had to align: location, legacy, and energy.

We signed the papers in silence. No champagne. No celebration.

Just a few deep breaths and a quiet nod to the journey it took to get there.

And then I walked out alone, onto the sand, the empty lot stretching in front of me. The skyline behind. The wind sharp. And I thought to myself: What are we really building here?

Not the villa. Not the valuation.

But the vibration.

The feeling people will have when they live here, walk here, and raise their children here.

Because we're not just building structures anymore.

We're shaping states of being.

And that's not something spreadsheets can measure.

But you feel it, in the corners of a room where sunlight rests just right, in the texture of the wood beneath your feet, in the quiet sense of safety a space gives you before you even realize it.

That's what Karma had become.

A mirror. A compass. A calling.

But it hadn't replaced Aethon.

It had revealed it.

Because even today, when I step into our shipping war room, glance at the movement charts, assess vessel positioning, fuel economics, and chartering trends, I feel alive. A different kind of alive. One that's elemental. Technical. Tactical.

Shipping remains my proving ground. It's where instinct meets algorithm. Where guts meet gravity. Where silence carries more weight than pitch decks.

There are days we negotiate deals that span five time zones, four currencies, and three levels of regulatory red tape. And we win, not because we shout, but because we listen better.

And when those deals close, I don't post about them.

I write about them in my notebook.

Because some victories are sacred.

They belong to the soul, not the scroll.

Just like some lessons are personal, even if they cost millions.

We've had deals that didn't deliver.

Partners who didn't align.

Markets that moved against us overnight.

But we never cursed those moments.

We studied them. Absorbed them.

Because there's no such thing as a wasted experience, only an unused one.

Every market collapse has taught me resilience.

Every team conflict has deepened my empathy.

Every wrong turn has sharpened my inner compass.

And that compass now guides everything.

Not just where we build.

But how we breathe.

I've started meditating before major negotiations.

I journal before strategy meetings.

Not to find the right words.

But to clear the noise.

Because clarity doesn't come from complexity. It comes from coherence.

And in an empire that spans shipping lanes, skylines, and soulwork, you need coherence more than charisma.

Today, when I meet young founders, they often ask: "What's the one piece of advice you'd give?"

I don't give advice.

I ask: "What part of you are you ignoring to build what you're building?"

Because that's usually the fracture.

They're building products, profits, personas, but ignoring the part of them that's whispering, This doesn't feel right.

That whisper?

That's the signal.

That's where reinvention begins.

And reinvention isn't a brand strategy. It's a spiritual one.

I've reinvented myself not by becoming someone new, but by remembering who I was before the world told me who to be.

Before KPIs.

Before capital.

Before corner offices and market cycles.

I was just a boy on a ship, staring at the horizon, knowing deep in his gut: There's more to build. But only if you're willing to build it differently.

And I still feel that boy inside me.

When I walk through construction sites.

When I troubleshoot ballast complications.

When I write new vision decks for Spectrum's next cohort.

He's still there.

Not wide-eyed anymore.

But watchful.

Not naïve.

But not cynical either.

He's learned that expansion isn't just what you add.

It's also what you shed.

The noise.

The fear.

The borrowed ambition.

Today, we're expanding again.

But with stillness.

We've entered wellness spaces, not just as an industry, but as a philosophy. We're studying biophilic design. Partnering with breathwork coaches. Exploring eco-sustainable resorts that function as healing ecosystems.

We're in early conversations about climate-focused shipping tech. Exploring emission models, hybrid vessel fuel frameworks, and AI-led maritime planning.

And I'm writing more. Not just notes. But blueprints for others, leaders navigating scale, founders facing solitude, and fathers trying to be present while building legacies.

This chapter of expansion is different.

Because now, we don't need to dominate.

We just need to align.

And in alignment, expansion is inevitable.

Because when vision and vibration sync, the map unfolds in ways no GPS can predict.

You meet people you never expected.

You receive resources you didn't plan for.

Doors open where there were only walls.

That's the terrain we're building now.

One where business is an act of service.

Where leadership is love with structure.

Where strategy is sacred geometry in motion.

And where growth isn't a destination.

It's a daily devotion.

To what's real.

To what matters.

To what lasts.

So, when people ask me today, "What's next?"

I don't give them a roadmap.

I just smile and say: We'll build the terrain as we walk it.

Because that's what real expansion is.

Not a plan.

A pilgrimage.

And the journey is just beginning.

Chapter 7: Leadership Reimagined - Intuition, Integrity, Impact

Leadership is commonly mistaken for a title. A destination. A chair at the table.

But to me, it has always been a rhythm.

A resonance. An energy that moves a room, even if no one sees it. You recognize a genuine leader by not what they say, but what they make people feel worthy of becoming around them.

I didn't learn to lead in management workshops or self-improvement books. I learned it in the quiet tension of lived experience, between silence and noise, victory and doubt. I learned it as a boy attempting to find room to grow in a house where love came with structure. I discovered it on the deck of ships lost in uncharted seas, where the only thing more tempestuous than the waves was the terror in my crew's eyes. And I discovered it later, in boardrooms, where ego, power, and performance metrics were poised to capsize the very human spirit we were supposed to enshrine.

Leadership, I've realized, doesn't always begin with clarity. Often, it begins with a deep discomfort. A dissonance with how things are. A quiet rejection of what the world expects of you. And then slowly, over years of listening to that dissonance and walking against the tide, something forms. A style. A voice. A way of showing up. That's what leadership has been for me, not an act of leading, but a practice of becoming.

Even as a kid, I knew I felt things deeply. I picked up on everything, the subtle change in tone when an adult replied with underlying irritation, the way a person's eyes would wander when they weren't all there, the uncertainty of someone's body when they wanted to say no but were too afraid. I did not know the words for all these things then. But I knew them. That sensitivity didn't always work for me; it made me irritable, fidgety, and too often misinterpreted. But eventually, I came to realize that what I possessed was a kind of emotional radar. A knowing. An instinct.

That instinct would eventually become the basis of how I governed. I didn't always have the numbers. But I had the trend. I didn't always have the facts. But I had the indication. And when your values and your instincts and your gut all overlap, it's extremely hard to make the wrong decision, even though others may take time to catch up.

But let's take a step back.

Leadership started with me in rebellion. Not the one that burns to the ground, but the one that questions others unquestioningly. At school, I was never the favourite of my teacher. I was not the neatest, the most compliant, or the one who nodded in agreement with each directive. I asked too many questions. I questioned authority, not because I was arrogant, but because I had to know. My grandfather, a disciplined and quiet force unto himself, once took me aside and told me, "You don't have to be heard to be heard. Power that speaks softly speaks last." That caught me, hidden somewhere deep down in my fire.

In some sense, I came into leadership in reverse. I didn't seek it out. I didn't want titles or attention. I was constantly more intrigued by building than showing up. In getting things to work better, smoother, and more deeply. And perhaps for that reason, people began following. Because they saw someone who was not acting out leadership, but embodying it.

At sea, the stakes were high and the tolerance for mistakes was hair-thin. Here, leadership wasn't theoretical; it was kill or be killed, fast or sink. You quickly discovered that screaming doesn't get scared men going. That experience does not always translate to wisdom. That calm is more valuable than speed.

I recall one night, in a tempestuous part of the ocean off the Suez Canal, our systems went dead in the middle of transit. No radar. No GPS. Complete power outage. My second officer stared at me, anticipating a direction. I just said, "We have practiced this." We went back to manual, relied on our bearings, and navigated the ship back on track. Afterwards, he informed me that he couldn't recall the orders, but he recalled the firmness in my voice. That was when I finally realized that leadership is not about always being in the know, it's about being steady when other people break.".

This principle followed me even when I walked off the boat and started to lead corporate teams. I took the same discipline, the same presence, into boardrooms filled with chatter. In those rooms, though, the dangers weren't storms or reefs, but politics, backroom deals, inflated egos. But the remedy was the same: Clarity. Calm. Conviction.

During those early years of corporate governance, I would normally be dealing with people who were older than me and already adept at the survival politics. I did not play the game. I never thought leadership was about domination. I questioned things that others would not dare question. I credited when credit was due. I owned up when others would not. And, respectively, it came, not because I demanded respect, but because I showed respect.

Nevertheless, I was not immune to ambition burnout. I drove myself relentlessly. Too relentlessly, at times. In an effort to show that performance and principles could work together, I pulled too far beyond what I could sustain. I went for months without seeing my family, sleeping little. I believed the solution to every issue was more work. But leadership is not about endurance. It's about understanding, of self, of system, of cycle. And it took me time, and a few wounds, to fully learn that lesson.

Years later, when I started to build my own companies, from Aethon to Karma and on, I finally had room to rethink leadership my own way. Not borrowed models. Not consultant lists. But a leadership built from scratch, from intuition, from hard-won wisdom, from spiritual congruence.

I didn't want performance teams. I wanted believing teams. Teams that felt safe, challenged, and committed to the purpose of our work. I hired them not for their skills, but for their soul. I observed how they reacted in pressure situations, how they respected service staff, and how they spoke when they didn't know anyone was watching.

A few of my best hires were individuals others had given up on, introverted, unpolished, even quirky. Yet I saw something in them, a hunger, a humility, a secret brilliance. I gave them space. I gave them trust. And they bloomed. Leadership, to me, was never about shaping people into perfection. It was about unleashing their natural rhythm.

Along the way, I gave up measuring leadership by results. I began measuring it by influence. Did the room become more stable when I walked in? Did my staff feel more clarity when they exited a meeting with me? Did I build more courage than confusion?

Mentoring new leaders turned out to bc one of the greatest sources of satisfaction for me. I never viewed it as a transaction. I didn't preach. I listened. I posed questions that demanded they stop. To dig deeper. To probe the root of their fears, their wants, and their aspirations. Most of them now head their own business, their own company. And I have a quiet pride, not that they cloned me, but that they became more themselves.

There is one protégé I recall very distinctly. He arrived at me raw, brilliant on paper, but filled with doubt in person. He second-guessed himself every time and doubted himself continually. I didn't attempt to repair him. I merely gave him a place where he might more clearly hear his own voice. I pushed him, yes. But I also spoke words of belief about him. His posture eventually shifted. His speech lost its hurried quality. His eyes gained confidence. Years afterward, he messaged me: "You didn't show me what to do. You reminded me of who I was." That is the greatest compliment I've ever received as a leader.

As I grew up in leadership, I found myself more and more motivated by questions that had nothing to do with reach or revenue. I began to ask, How does it feel to work here? What unspoken tensions lie within our teams? Are we growing quickly, or merely getting louder? And most of all, are we holding on to why we began?

These weren't questions that you could answer in meetings or memos. They asked for more listening, the kind of listening you can only have in quiet, with your ego put aside. So I started making more room for that quiet. I began getting to the office early just to sit in silence before the day got started. I'd pace the floor without an agenda, just to feel the energy. I'd take one-on-one meetings outside the boardroom, on long walks, over quiet coffee, and I'd ask questions that had nothing to do with performance metrics.

Over time, I realised something profound: true leadership is more about tuning in than speaking up. It's about presence. And presence is not about charisma. It's about coherence, when your words, actions, and energy all say the same thing. That coherence becomes your culture.

At Karma, this was one of our core values. We didn't create the company based on a service or product. We created it based on a vibration. A feeling that real estate could have a soul. That leadership could have softness without diminishing strength. That performance and presence could exist together.

Folks would ask why our retention rate was so high, why our partners never defaulted, and why we never had to pursue headlines or hype to raise capital. I'd reply with a smile, "Because we don't operate out of fear." And I wasn't kidding.

We didn't respond to markets. We reacted to meaning. Every acquisition, every hire, every pivot was not just done by intuition, but by integrity.

Integrity, to me, is the currency of leadership. And it's not usually about the great moral choices. It appears in the tiny moments, how you respond to disappointment, how you speak about the competition, how you show up when nobody's looking. I've had times when it was easier to walk away from a multi-million-dollar opportunity than to say yes to something that wasn't aligned. Not because I had a plan B, but because I had a backbone.

I recall one project in Eastern Europe, a beautiful site, high margins, ideal optics. But something wasn't right. The local dynamics were unclear. The process was hurried. I couldn't locate the source of my discomfort on paper, but my gut shouted. So I walked away. We let the deal go. Some labeled it as idiotic. Six months after that, the same project was at the center of legal and environmental disputes. We had dodged a bullet, not through diligence, but through discernment.

And that's the other layer of leadership that doesn't get talked about enough: discernment. The ability to read what isn't being said. To sense what's behind the numbers. To trust that your inner signals are as important as the external ones. In today's data-saturated world, it's easy to drown in dashboards and ignore your own compass. But every time I've done that, every time I've let logic override my instinct, I've paid the price.

There was this shipping business in Southeast Asia that seemed ideal on paper. The figures were good. The partners decent. The route under-exploited. But there was something about the tone of the first few meetings that didn't ring true, felt forced, edgy, a bit theatrical, too rehearsed. Against my better judgment, I approved. Six months in, things started to crack. The leadership was not aligned. The ethics were dodgy. And we had to leave, incurring both reputational and financial damage. That error was not a miscalculation; it was a lack of trust in my own instinct.

I don't beat myself up for those instances. They remind me I am human. They also hone my edge. Leadership is never perfect. It's return. Return on emotional equity, return on physical toll, return on investment of one's self. How fast you return to your centre. How you navigate the pain, but don't park there. How you learn, reset, and move.

The hardest lesson that I had to learn was about people. I've always been a believer in people. Too much at times. I've supported individuals who were visionary but not on the same values. Who could articulate a vision but did not have values. Who delivered tremendous short-term outcomes but wrought long-term havoc along the way.

Releasing those individuals wasn't simple. I don't fire. I invest. I develop. I hope. But I've come to realize that one toxic player can save you ten garbage players. Culture is not established by charm. Culture is established by consistency. And the instant somebody compromises that with poison, I respond, not in anger, but in clarity.

I once had a senior partner who impressed everyone. Fantastic speaker, brilliant mind, excellent network. But over time, I started to see something amiss. The team would get nervous in his presence. Information was being withheld. Errors were being covered up. And the general vibe took a hit when he entered the room. I spoke to him about it lightly, on several occasions. Provided support, coaching, and time. But the conduct didn't change. Sooner or later, I made the decision. I asked him to step aside.

It was ugly. Expensive. Politically charged. But within a matter of weeks, the whole system took a collective deep breath. Productivity improved. Smiles reappeared. That's when I knew: I had made the correct choice. Not for the business. For the people. And in the end, those two are one.

There's another element of leadership that doesn't get discussed often: vulnerability. Not performative vulnerability, the kind you package for a keynote. But real, raw, unguarded truth.

I've tearfully broken down in front of my team. I've owned up to blunders in town halls. I've recounted my darkest moments of doubt with junior employees. Not because I wanted to be perceived as emotional, but because I wanted to be perceived as human. And in doing so, I let others know it was okay to be human too.

One of my strongest memories was at a leadership offsite back in the early Karma days. We were thinking through vision and growth strategies, and someone blurted out, "What are you most fearful of at this moment?" I blurted out without thinking, "To lose myself in success." The room fell silent. And one by one, the others began to open up. Not plans. But stories. Fears. Truths. That night, we didn't create a blueprint. We created a connection.

And that connection became the foundation upon which everything we've accomplished since was built.

And then there was a period, when Karma was on the ascendancy and my property gambles were multiplying, when the world around me began changing rapidly. Appreciation increased. Invitations came in bulk. Clapping became thunderous. And ego, that age-old seducer, began knocking at my door. It manifested itself in little things at first. My tolerance lessened. My demands shot up. I grew impatient during meetings. Less attentive to the family. More concerned with scaling than serving. It didn't survive long, perhaps a couple of months. But it was long enough to teach me the price of disconnection.

One evening, after a particularly biting exchange with a trusted aide, I sat in my study by myself and asked myself a question I had not asked in years: "Why did I begin this? "

The response wasn't growth. It was grace.

And the minute I remembered that, everything changed again.

I returned to old habits: early morning walks, silent journaling, and unstructured time with my daughter. I ceased aggressive hiring. I rejected speaking engagements. I revisited our hiring processes, our KPIs, and even our internal document language.

I didn't just take the business back into alignment.

I took myself back.

That's what reimagined leadership demands.

Not simply vision. But vigilance.

Not just common sense. But integrity.

Not just influence. But peace of mind.

And as time has passed, I have less and less of that feeling, that the task is a mountain to climb, and more and more a circle to walk around in, where, at each step, you get to go back to point one, a step or two further and richer and wiser.

As my businesses grew, so did my function. I was no longer the day-to-day director. I was now the architect, the individual who no longer places every brick, but who prescribes the angles, the load-bearing beams, the light that must come in through each window. And in that transformation, I learned the art of leadership at a distance.

Leading remotely is harder than leading from the centre. It requires more trust, better communication, and clearer boundaries. You must learn to delegate not only tasks, but vision. To empower without micromanaging. To inspire without being seen all the time.

I needed to become highly deliberate about the people I surrounded myself with. I started building leadership teams for chemistry, not comfort. I did not want yes-men. I wanted truth-tellers. People who would challenge me with respect. Who could notice my blind spots and still have faith in the direction we were headed.

The quality of your inner circle determines the altitude of your leadership.

That became my golden rule.

So I began selecting differently.

I sought out individuals who didn't require managing. Who were self-directed, self-reflected, and could direct others with elegance. I interviewed individuals not for what they had accomplished, but for how they had accomplished it. I listened for language, were they communicating out of ego or out of experience? Out of defensiveness or out of depth?

One of the finest leaders I ever employed was a woman who'd been rejected by three companies for being "too introverted." But as soon as I met her, I knew she was there. Not boisterous, not put together, but sharp. She didn't say much, but when she did, the room changed. Within six months, she'd turned around one of our most stuck verticals, not by charm, but by clarity. She now leads a team of eighty. Quietly. Powerfully. Without ever lifting her voice.

That's when I realized: leadership isn't about personality. It's about energy. Some leaders arrive with volume. Others with silence. But the great ones arrive with impact.

And impact is never an accident.

It's the result of alignment between what you do and who you are. Between your values and your vision.

This alignment became my bottom line.

In each company that I worked with, Karma, Aethon, ZENA, Silkleaf, and Spectrum, I instilled a philosophy of leadership based on alignment. We don't only reward performance, we reward presence. We don't only promote output, we promote ownership. We don't hire because of pedigree, we hire because of potential, and willingness to grow in the fire.

I recall a conversation with one of the mid-level managers who asked me, "How do you define leadership success?" My response caught him off guard. I replied, "By how people talk about you when you're not in the room. And how they feel about themselves when they are."

That's it.

That's the whole game.

Because leadership isn't a solo act.

It's an ecosystem.

And every decision you make, every email, every interaction, every pause or presence, ripples through that ecosystem. Either towards harmony, or away from it.

I've made it a practice over the years to walk into various teams unexpectedly. Not to audit, but to soak. I quietly sit in the back of a meeting. I observe body language. I see how people talk to one another. How they deal with disagreement. And from that, I have a truer sense of the health of the team than any quarterly report could provide.

Culture isn't written. It's felt.

And as a leader, you are always writing culture, even in silence.

There were moments when I didn't get it right. Moments when I allowed performance to justify poor behavior. When I pushed hard conversations into the latter. When I accepted toxicity for the sake of results.

But each time I cut culture short, it came back and bit me. Sometimes in attrition. Sometimes in misalignment. Sometimes in slow, silent disengagement.

That's when I realized I'd lose a genius but not keep a misaligned one. Because talent misaligned is turbulence in the making.

I've lost great minds. People I enjoyed, even admired. But whose energy broke the system. And each time, it pained. But each time, it healed the company.

That's the bitter taste of leadership: sacrificing short-term harmony for long-term harmony. Doing what's right, though it's hard. And standing alone when the way is clear, but unpopular.

There's another aspect of leadership I've leaned into more heavily over the last few years: mentoring by modelling.

I once thought that leadership was a matter of leading people through speech. But now I think it's a matter of living what you want others to become.

When I set boundaries, others feel that they can set theirs.

When I am willing to admit error, others feel comfortable admitting theirs.

When I am consistently present, others adjust to that rhythm.

You don't motivate people by teaching them. You motivate by being the evidence.

And that's not always glamorous. Sometimes it's about keeping quiet in a room where you could have the floor. Sometimes it's about being blamed for something that wasn't necessarily your fault. Sometimes it's about holding space for someone else's development even when your own feels unclear.

Leadership is service.

It's really about assisting others to rise, even if that means stepping back.

One of the biggest things I've done as a leader is to establish a ritual of exit interviews, not merely when an employee leaves the company, but when they leave a project, a role, or a significant phase. I sit down with them and I say, "What would we have done differently to allow you to flourish?"

Not to place blame. But to learn. To listen. To evolve.

Some of the most powerful insights about our companies have come from these quiet, post-mortem conversations. Because people are more honest when they're no longer afraid of consequences. And that honesty is a gift.

It's helped me redesign onboarding, restructure incentives, and reframe our leadership expectations.

It's reminded me that leadership isn't just about creating high-performing environments. It's about creating humane ones.

Where people don't just succeed, they belong.

And that sense of belonging starts at the top.

If you desire a culture of trust, you must be trustworthy.

If you desire people to care, you must demonstrate that you care.

If you desire innovation, you must build psychological safety.

And that starts with you.

With how you show up.

With the energy you bring.

With the mirror you hold.

The more I was in charge, the more I realized that leadership doesn't scale through systems. Leadership scales through belief. You can put all the tools, dashboards, and processes in place, but if people do not believe in what they are doing, they will never give you their total self. They might turn up. But they won't show up.

Belief, I realized, is the unseen infrastructure of any organisation.

It's what keeps people in the dark. What propels them through skepticism. What causes them to remain even when alternatives are more convenient.

And purpose gives rise to faith.

So I set out to make it my top priority that each vertical, each venture, each team had a definitive understanding of why they were there, above revenue, above growth, above KPIs.

For Karma, it was sanctuaries, not buildings.

For Aethon, it was about ethical shipping, discipline over disruption.

For ZENA, it was about feminine energy in function, elegance with edge.

For Spectrum, it was about future-proofing talent, not just placing it.

For Silkleaf, it was about securing legacy, not just growing capital.

Once that clarity emerged, decisions became easier. Culture became cleaner. And growth became more sustainable, because it was rooted, not rushed.

That simplicity also redesigned the way I managed conflict.

Early on in my leadership years, I saw conflict as something to be avoided or put out quickly. But over time, I realized that it was a doorway, an entrance to greater understanding, unspoken needs, and hidden truth.

Conflict, when handled gently, shows character.

I've had tough talks with co-founders, family members, and even long-time friends. Talks that were like crossroads. But I never went into them with an agenda to win. I went into them with a plan to listen. To look beyond the problem and see the person. To try to understand what fear or wound could be behind the behaviour.

That mindset, that move from reaction to reflection, changed everything.

It made me less defensive. More discerning. And more surprisingly decisive.

Because when you're clear within, you don't have to control out.

One was during a transition at Karma. We were reorganizing the leadership structure, and one of our senior executives, a person I highly respected, felt displaced. He came to me visibly upset. The old me might have clarified the reason behind the move, legitimized it, and tried to rationalize it all away.

But this time, I simply listened.

Not to reply. But to get it.

And along the way in that conversation, the temperature changed. He didn't require answers. He required seeing. He required to be seen. And once he was, the alignment reestablished itself.

Another silent leadership truth: Most tensions melt away when people feel truly seen.

Recognition isn't awards or applause. It's about showing up. About the moment you look somebody in the face and say, "I value you." Not as a resource. But as a human being.".

In all our companies, I've made it a point to institutionalise informal gratitude. Weekly notes of appreciation. Public acknowledgments in team calls. Celebrating small wins, not just milestones. Because these tiny acts, done consistently, build a culture of care.

And when care becomes culture, excellence follows naturally.

There is also a deeper spiritual aspect to leadership that I've learned to embrace, particularly in the last few years. As Karma expanded, as our portfolio grew larger, as our impact reached across borders, I felt drawn toward inner anchoring.

Success without soul is a silent tragedy.

So I started to slow down. To meditate more. To seek not only advisors, but astrologers, spiritual guides, and even energy practitioners. Not for making decisions, but for clarity. For alignment. For deeper listening.

Some will say it's unconventional. I say it's necessary.

Because leadership isn't just outer work. It's inner work reflected outward.

The more you understand your triggers, the fewer you create.

The more deeply you're aware, the more expansive your impact is.

The more grounded your centre is, the more focused your circumference.

And in an acceleration-addicted world, that focus is your competitive edge.

It's also your healing space.

Throughout my years, I've had team members approach me not only with business issues, but with personal emergencies. Health crises. Family crises. Times of intense emotional upheaval.

I don't advise them. I don't attempt to solve.

I simply hold space.

And to me, that is also leadership.

To be a safe space, not a strategic brain.

To hold not only vision, but empathy.

To remind people that ambition does not mean emotional abandonment.

Some of my most impactful leadership moments occurred in silence. A pat on the shoulder. An extended pause during a tough meeting. A coffee shared after a loss.

Because when people are looking back, they don't even recall your slides and speeches.

They recall how you made them feel at the moment it counted.

That's the legacy of presence.

And it is the only one I wish to leave behind.

I remember during one particularly difficult period, when we were between a multi-country legal problem that had reputational risk as well as financial stress, when I was alone, standing on a rooftop in Dubai, looking down at the lights on the city. It was midnight already. My phone was full of messages I hadn't gotten around to reading. My calendar, booked up for the next ten days.

But in that quiet, I experienced a surge of peace. Because I knew we'd survive.

Not because we were the most funded. Not because we knew all the answers.

But because we had something stronger: alignment. Throughout the leadership. Throughout the vision. Throughout the energy.

And when alignment is present, resilience is inevitable.

You don't break. You calibrate.

You don't panic. You pivot.

You don't merely survive. You sculpt new strength.

That rooftop became a metaphor for me.

A reminder that leadership isn't about standing above the chaos.

It's about standing still within it, and still seeing clearly.

As I reflect on the trajectory of my leadership, I see that the most defining changes did not issue from boardrooms or wars won. They issued from breakdowns. From burnouts. From moments of wondering not only if I'd made the right decisions, but if I was on the right path.

There was a point when all seemed well on paper, but something did not feel right inside. We were growing rapidly. Deals were closing. Investors were hot. And I would come home, look at my desk late at night, and get this inner emptiness.

It wasn't exhaustion. It was a separation.

I had allowed the numbers to dictate the significance. And in that, I had lost my way from the very reason it began, the passion to build with heart.

That wake-up call had a profound impact.

I started peeling back the noise. Delegating more frequently. Saying no more frequently. Creating larger gaps between decisions. Swapping speed for intention. Defining success not only in terms of what we created, but in how we felt creating it.

That transition, from performance to presence, changed not only my leadership but my life.

I started living more clearly. More spacious. More effortless.

I quit chasing importance and began to enrich richness.

I quit proving and began to be.

And in that space, a new form of leadership was born, one that was not reactive, but responsive. Not fueled by fear, but rooted in trust.

This is what I now refer to as "energetic leadership."

Where each meeting, each milestone, and each message is steeped in the clarity of state.

Where your strategy isn't followed by people, it's felt.

And when your state is clear, calm, and clean, the whole system comes into coherence.

It's not philosophy. It's physics.

Energy is infectious.

Enter a room stressed, and you'll induce chaos.

Enter the room grounded, and you establish coherence.

I started using this principle in everything, from how we designed our office areas to the format of our meetings.

Meetings now start with a breath. Not because it's cool, but because it works.

When we start with presence, we make better choices.

When we respect silence, we hear what is most important.

When we slow down, we move ahead more quickly.

These little rituals became the blueprint of culture.

They established a rhythm that others could sync with. A cadence that was safe, clear, and directed. And over time, that rhythm became our competitive advantage.

While most leaders were burning out, we were burning brighter.

Not because we were working harder, but because we were working right.

We were not scaling chaos. We were scaling coherence.

And that's what true leadership does.

It doesn't just guide. It grounds. It balances.

Another change I made was to my ego. In the beginning years, I needed to be everywhere. To be heard. To be seen. But as I grew older, I came to understand, the less ego, the better I performed.

I began to take a step back in meetings. Talking less in conversations. Asking more questions than providing answers. And each time I did, something remarkable occurred; others emerged.

They started to own the room. They started to introduce ideas I had never considered. They started to lead.

And that, I came to understand, is the true aim of leadership: to make yourself progressively unnecessary, but infinitely powerful.

Not by doing less. But doing differently.

This was starkly apparent when Mridula started running ZENA more autonomously. I saw her make decisions I would not have made, but that worked. Not because they were improved or inferior. But because they were hers.

That made me learn something very powerful: leadership is not about duplication. It's about realization.

Assisting others to realize their own voice, their own beat, their own leadership DNA.

That is what mentorship is.

It's not about leaving trails for others to tread.

It's about giving them the strength to follow their own path, with purpose and certainty.

Even with my son Niranjan, I've done so.

I don't teach. I watch. I ponder. I build space for his mind to expand, for his questions to be honored, for his mistakes not to be penalized but analyzed.

I'm not bringing up a copy. I'm bringing up a sovereign.

And that, too, is leadership.

Parenting is leadership. Marriage is leadership. Self-care is leadership.

Because in all of them, you are either opening yourself up or closing down into old habits.

The choice is always yours.

Others have asked me: "What's the one skill every leader needs to become expert at?"

My response is straightforward. Listening.

Deep, conscious, unflustered listening.

Not listening to reply. Listening to comprehend.

To what is spoken, what is unspoken, and what is felt.

Because in every conversation, there's a truth attempting to surface. And the more present you are, the more clearly you'll hear it.

A few of my most life-changing decisions were made in silence.

Not because someone presented a compelling argument.

But because something in my gut said, "This is it."

That sort of clarity only happens when your internal noise is low.

When your ego isn't in charge.

When your agenda isn’t louder than your awareness.

And that’s the work of a leader.

Not just to set direction, but to clear the distortion.

To be a tuning fork for truth.

Even when it’s inconvenient.

Even when it’s unpopular.

Especially then.

The farther I’ve travelled in this journey, from ship decks to boardrooms, from asset acquisitions to energy alignment, the more I’ve realised one truth: the highest form of leadership is self-leadership.

Because when you learn to lead yourself through uncertainty, through exhaustion, through loss, through re-creation, no storm outside can really rattle you.

And that self-leadership is not created in ease.

It's created in fire.

In ambiguity.

In those darkest, most isolated hours when nobody's looking, yet you still decide to present with authenticity.

There were nights I doubted it all, my way, my kind, my speed. Moments when a bad bargain threatened to bring down a company, or when treachery from someone I trusted stung harder than any loss of money. There were seasons when I was lonelier than I'd ever say out loud.

But those seasons taught me toughness beyond stubbornness.

They taught me forgiveness.

To mend faster. To bounce back more tenderly. To come back stronger.

They also showed me that power is not dominant; it's in submission.

Not the submission of losing.

But the submission of having faith in the process.

Faith that what's meant to be yours won't come past you.

That every setback has its plan.

That every detour is just part of a longer map you haven't been shown yet.

And in submission, I learned the greatest leadership of all, spiritual leadership.

Not mystical. Not religious.

But the type that establishes itself in values so profound, they become your GPS navigating any mist.

The type that enables you to construct empires without hardening your heart.

The type that enables you to exercise power without being taken over by it.

The type that reminds you: you're not your title, your achievement, your bottom line.

You're the space out of which all of it emerges.

And once I realized that, I started leading differently.

I started respecting silence at the table, for oftentimes the greatest answers arise in pause.

I started blessing each project we embarked on, not in ritual, but in intention.

I started thanking my team frequently, not out of duty, but out of reverence.

For I knew: without them, this vision would never materialize.

And gradually, that energy turned contagious.

Clients began saying to us: "There's something different about the way you do business."

Vendors were saying: "It feels lighter, easier, clearer working with your teams."

New hires were saying: "I feel like I've found my place."

That was when I realized we were no longer merely building companies.

We were building cultures.

We were sending energy.

We were rewriting what great leadership could look like.

Not just smart. But genuine.

Not just efficient. But caring.

Not just creative. But integrous.

And the ripple of that extended far, far beyond any bottom line.

Because when you lead with depth, your legacy becomes unstoppable.

Not in buildings. But in beliefs.

Not in deals. But in dignity.

Not in fame. But in frequency, the frequency you leave behind in every room, every relationship, every outcome.

That is the leadership I want to live. That is the leadership I want to teach. That is the kind of leadership I want my son to see, not in speeches, but in my stillness.

Because at the end of it all, when the meetings are over and the light fades, the only question that really counts is: Did I lead with love? Did I build with alignment? Did I honour my compass? Did I leave people better than I found them?

If the answer is yes, even on most days, then I've succeeded. Then the companies will outgrow me. The teams will outperform me. The name will erode. But the spirit, that soft, powerful spirit of what it means to lead from the soul, will persist.

In every wall we constructed with intent.

In every vessel we navigated with faith.

In every life we impacted with integrity.

Because real leadership isn't shouting.

It's lived.

And if I've done that even a little, then this journey, with all its storms and stillness, has been worth it.

Chapter 8: The Moments of Giving Back to the Community

At some stage of every journey, the clatter of success is hushed, and you hear a different voice, an older voice that towers above ambition and is more thunderous than applause.

The voice which says not, "What have you gained", but, "What have you given."

My moment was not celebrated by a trophy or a news article. It came in silence, on a late evening walk, away from deals and spreadsheets, as the sun dipped below the skyline of Dubai. I paused and realised I wasn't walking forward. I was circling back. Back to the young boy from a small town in India, with no access, no backup plan, just the stubbornness to rise.

I had climbed, yes. But now it was time to reach.

I never built my journey to be admired from a distance. I built it so that someone else could look at it and say, "If he could, maybe I can." That may be what matters. That opening of possibility.

Because leadership, to me, isn't complete until it becomes circular. You rise, and then you rise again, but this time, with someone else on your shoulders.

And that is where true impact begins.

Giving back, for me, isn't an act. It's a memory. It is remembering that feeling, wanting someone to help, and not knowing who to turn to. It is the pain of rejection, of wondering just once, of that feeling of hope being shuttered because you are too young, too new, too ambitious. It is a recollection of all I was told, no, and deciding to be the yes of someone.

To me, mentorship is not a weekend undertaking. It is not passion. It is a vow I made to myself when I came aboard my first ship, not knowing whether I was ever going to fit there or not. When I would find my voice, I said to myself, I would use it to echo somebody else nearby.

And that voice has never left me.

I've mentored cadets who didn't know the difference between port and starboard. I've reviewed business models scribbled on paper napkins in crowded coffee shops. I've taken midnight calls from aspiring entrepreneurs who had no roadmap, just raw conviction.

And in each of those conversations, I saw a piece of my past.

I didn't always have a mentor. But I had moments. Moments of grace from strangers. Moments of clarity born from failure. Moments when the right person gave me a word, a warning, or a window. Those moments shaped me. So today, I create them, intentionally.

Not all the people I've helped made it to the headlines. Some didn't even launch. But they learned. And for some, that was enough. Because sometimes, the best thing you can do for someone is not to help them win, but to help them wait. To help them see that delay is not denial, and that failure is not fatal.

I remember one young founder from Gujarat. He came to me, decked in enthusiasm, with a pitch that was more emotion than execution. He had borrowed money from friends and was already two months into operations. The model was flawed. The numbers didn't add up. But his fire was real.

I didn't dismiss him. I didn't sugarcoat either. I sat him down and deconstructed the plan and took it bit by bit, and explained to him why it would not work. He went away, seriously shaken, disappointed, maybe resentful. However, it took two years before he made his comeback. Same fire. New model. Leaner, keener, wiser. This time, I not only supported him by counsel, but also by giving him access. Today, his venture has grown fivefold, not because I gave him money, but because I gave him a mirror, the one that showed him what needed to change before the world would say yes.

That's what mentorship is. It's not always motivation. Sometimes, it's an interruption.

You interrupt someone's fantasy with truth. You interrupt their echo chamber with perspective. You interrupt their urgency with patience. And in doing so, you don't dim their dream, you make it real.

There was another young man, a former seafarer like me, who reached out from Sharjah. He had been laid off, was struggling to make ends meet, and had an idea for a crew management service. He didn't have the capital. He didn't have the polish. But he had scars. Real ones. And scars, I've found, make for the best teachers.

I didn't invest in his company. I invested in his learning. I connected him with a few key partners, gave him a six-month roadmap, and checked in every fortnight. Today, his company manages offshore staffing for three global firms. He still calls me "Captain" with reverence, but I remind him, "You're the captain now."

And that's the joy. To step back. To see someone find their own wind.

Philanthropy, too, is something I approach not as charity, but as clarity. I ask myself: where can one act create a thousand ripples?

Through the Karma Foundation, we've done small things. But in the right places, they became big.

We've paid school fees for children in villages where dropout rates were soaring. We've sent bicycles to girls who walked 7 km to school every day. We've funded skill programs that helped women turn backyard pickles into packaged businesses.

It's not glamorous. It doesn't make the papers. But I've seen a smile on a grandmother's face when her granddaughter put on a school uniform for the first time. That smile is worth more than any ROI.

In Dubai, where glitz often overshadows grit, I've focused on giving time. Time to university students trying to break into real estate. Time to first-generation founders without networks. Time to junior team members to figure out what kind of leader they want to be.

Sometimes, a single conversation changes the trajectory of a person. I've seen it happen. I've felt the weight of it, when someone says, "That thing you said three years ago, it stayed with me."

That's why I show up. That's why I give.

Because money may build walls, but words build worlds.

And I want to leave behind a world where ambition is not a privilege, but a possibility.

One of the most humbling moments of my career wasn't an IPO or an award. It happened in Singapore, during a casual alumni meet of former mariners. I was invited to speak, just a short talk on entrepreneurship and transition. I spoke from the heart, about the shift from command to culture, from sea to startup.

Afterward, a few senior officers came to me, grey-haired, seasoned, some I had admired from afar. They didn't just praise the talk. They thanked me. One said, "Years ago, I almost invested in a venture that would have wiped out my retirement savings. You told me not to. I didn't believe you then. But I followed your advice. And today, I'm still standing."

That moment hit me hard.

Because what you prevent quietly is often more powerful than what you enable loudly.

I've always believed that giving is not about having abundance. It's about recognising responsibility.

Responsibility to your past. Responsibility to your privilege. And most of all, responsibility to your power, the power to influence, to shape, to uplift. And when you truly internalise that, giving no longer feels like an act of generosity. It feels like breathing. Natural. Necessary.

In the business world, I've seen people calculate their giving the way they calculate tax. As a deduction. An obligation. But for me, the real ROI of giving is never in numbers. It's in nights slept better. In letters received years later. In people who go on to build lives because you gave them a bridge when they only had water beneath their feet.

I remember once, during the early days of Karma Developers, we had just closed a major deal in Dubai. It was a turning point, financially and emotionally. A win that had come after months of tireless effort. My team suggested a celebration, and we booked a quiet dinner. But I remember leaving halfway.

Not because I wasn't happy. But because my mind was elsewhere.

That same week, I had received a letter from a school principal in rural Uttar Pradesh. A batch of girl students, top scorers in their class, were about to drop out because they couldn't afford uniforms, transportation, or even sanitary pads.

That letter haunted me more than any balance sheet ever had.

The next day, I flew to India. Quietly. No PR. No entourage. I met the principal. I met the girls. I met their parents. And I didn't just write a cheque. I sat with them. I heard their stories. I listened.

Some of those girls went on to finish school. One got into nursing. Another began training in a tailoring unit we later funded. None of them may remember my name five years from now. But I'll remember their eyes, that flicker of possibility rekindled.

And that, to me, is the essence of real giving.

It's not about being remembered. It's about remembering who you were before the world remembered you.

The Karma Foundation wasn't born from strategy. It was born from sleepless nights. Nights when I lay awake wondering why I had been spared, spared the misfortunes, spared the tragedies, spared the ceilings that so many others faced. I realised that maybe I wasn't spared. I was selected to be a vessel. A bridge. A compass.

Today, through the foundation, we've built more than interventions. We've built belief.

In one district alone, we piloted a youth skilling program that taught solar panel installation to unemployed young men. Some had never stepped out of their village. Today, two of them are working in energy companies in the Gulf. Another one returned to start a small repair unit. Their lives changed. But more importantly, they changed the stories being told in their communities.

That ripple is what drives me.

Because I know what it means to feel unseen. To be told that your dreams are too big for your background. To hear laughter when you speak your vision. And to still, somehow, keep going.

That's why, even in Dubai, I've created quiet support systems. I've offered internships to students with no references. I've opened doors in real estate and shipping to young Indians and Pakistanis who grew up believing those industries were beyond their reach.

I remember one young man who interned with Karma for just six months. He barely spoke during meetings, always stood in the back, but observed everything. At the end of his tenure, he came to me with a handwritten note. In it, he said, "Sir, I used to think men like you only existed in Forbes magazines. But you made me believe that I could belong in those rooms too."

I still have that note.

It reminds me that presence is the greatest present.

That showing up, listening, mentoring, guiding, even for a moment, can light a fire that lasts a lifetime.

And sometimes, giving back isn't about lifting someone from poverty. Sometimes it's about saving them from a mistake.

Over the years, I've had dozens of entrepreneurs come to me with pitches. Some were brilliant. Others were beautiful disasters waiting to happen. I've said no more often than yes, not because I didn't believe in them, but because I believed in something deeper: their potential beyond that particular idea.

I've walked founders through financial models, dissected risks, and pointed out blind spots. And I've had uncomfortable conversations, the kind where someone leaves upset, thinking you didn't get their vision.

But time has a way of revealing intention.

Many of them came back later, thanking me for not indulging their enthusiasm at the cost of their future. One of them, now running a successful agritech platform, told me, "You didn't invest in my startup. But you saved me from mortgaging my father's land. That was the bigger gift."

That line still sits heavy on my heart.

Because there's a quiet kind of giving, the kind where you don't write a cheque, but you rewrite someone's path.

Of course, not all my efforts have gone as planned. There have been disappointments. Ventures I supported that folded. Students who dropped out despite our help. Individuals who took our support and vanished. That's the reality of impact work. It's not a straight line. It's a messy mosaic of attempts, learnings, and quiet resilience.

But I never stopped.

Because the few who rise make it worth it.

People often ask me why I keep studying, why I pursue degrees and certifications even now. My answer is simple: I study not to climb higher, but to pull stronger.

Knowledge, for me, is not ego. It's empathy. The more I know, the more I can teach. The more I understand, the more I can simplify. I've done MBAs, a Master of Laws, a PhD, certifications across finance, audit, risk, and even aviation. Not for LinkedIn. But for life.

So that when a founder walks in with a pitch in blockchain, or a mother calls me asking about higher education options for her daughter, I can guide them not just with opinion, but with depth.

Because guidance is not about answers. It's about anchoring someone in awareness.

And when that awareness clicks, when a mentee finally sees their own blind spot, when a student finds their voice, when a young woman dares to dream beyond her postcode, that is my dividend.

I don't believe in inheritance. I believe in imparting. In passing on more than money. In transferring values, frameworks, and mindsets.

In India, we often talk about karma. But karma isn't just what you do. It's what you enable. What you amplify. What you prevent.

Every act of giving is a karmic seed. Some bloom instantly. Some take years. But none are wasted.

I remember during COVID, when things were uncertain and everyone was holding tight to resources, I made a different choice. We increased our philanthropy budget. We launched emergency healthcare grants. We paid salaries to small vendors. We extended credit to our tenants.

People called it risky. I called it responsible.

Because the world doesn't just test your resilience. It tests your resolve to remain human when it's inconvenient.

Today, as I reflect, I don't measure my success by the towers I've built or the ships I've owned. I measure it by the bridges I've created, between fear and faith, between doubt and doing, between what was and what could be.

Those bridges don't carry my name. But they carry my fingerprint.

And that is enough.

Sometimes, giving doesn't look like charity. It looks like patience.

Like staying on a phone call with a distraught first-time founder at midnight as he questions every decision he's made. Like reviewing a strategy deck line by line for someone who can't afford a professional consultant. Like holding space for someone who doesn't need advice, they just need not to feel alone.

I've had countless such conversations.

One young woman, a tech entrepreneur in her twenties, reached out via LinkedIn. She was on the verge of shutting down her startup. Burned through her savings, rejected by investors, the co-founder had walked away. Something in her message struck me. Not the desperation, but the dignity.

I agreed to a 30-minute call.

We spoke for nearly two hours.

Not about capital. But about clarity.

I asked her what she truly wanted, beyond the product, beyond the metrics. What was the itch that wouldn't let her sleep? What version of her life did she see when the noise died down?

She didn't have answers then. But that call lit something in her.

Six months later, she launched a leaner, more focused version of her idea. This time with a co-founder who complemented her, not competed with her. Last I heard, they had secured seed funding and were onboarding paying customers.

I never spoke about that conversation publicly.

Because real mentorship doesn't happen on stage. It happens in silence.

It happens in the unnoticed spaces, after the Zoom ends, when the hope is fading, when the person on the other side doesn't need motivation. They need meaning.

And sometimes, it's about presence more than perspective.

In my office, there's no formal mentorship program. But people know: if they knock, I'll open. If they ask, I'll share. Not because I know everything, but because I know what it feels like to have no one to ask.

Even my own leadership team, seasoned as they are, knows that I don't operate from a pedestal. I mentor sideways. I walk beside. I share mistakes as openly as I share wins.

I tell them how I once hired a senior executive purely on instinct, charmed by charisma, swayed by credentials. Within months, we discovered financial mismanagement. It took years to repair the damage, not just monetarily, but emotionally. The betrayal of trust cut deeper than the cost.

That experience taught me to value alignment over appearance.

It also taught me the power of truth, hard, uncomfortable, unvarnished truth.

So now, when I guide others, I don't sugarcoat. I don't protect their feelings at the cost of their future. I challenge them, push them, reflect them back to themselves. And the ones who rise? They're not just grateful. They're transformed.

Over the years, I've watched my mentees become mentors themselves.

One of the most fulfilling moments came when a former cadet, now a shipping executive, called to ask for advice, not for himself, but for a junior he was mentoring.

That's the ripple.

That's when you know your impact is not linear, it's exponential.

You didn't just lift someone. You created a lifter.

And yet, I never plan these moments. I never set KPIs for kindness.

The universe has its own calculus for impact. I just try to stay available.

Recently, someone asked me at a panel: "What's the most generous thing you've ever done?"

I smiled.

Because the truth is, the most generous thing I've ever done is not a thing.

It's a way of being.

It's choosing to lead with heart when it's easier to lead with hierarchy.

It's choosing to teach when you could just transact.

It's choosing to care when no one is watching.

And most of all, it's choosing to give when you're still healing.

Yes, giving requires resources. But more than that, it requires resolve.

It's easy to give when you've made it. But what about when you're still in the climb?

What about when you yourself are bruised, uncertain, stretched thin?

That's when giving becomes not a gesture, but a philosophy.

I've donated while downsizing.

Mentored while grieving.

Supported others' dreams while mine were still under construction.

Because I've always believed: the world doesn't wait for you to be perfect before you contribute.

You give what you can, where you can, as you are.

And sometimes, your very imperfection becomes someone else's permission.

One of my favorite stories is of a boy in Ghaziabad. His father was a driver. His mother cleaned homes. But he had a spark, sharp, driven, unpolished but pure. Someone from our team flagged his name during a scholarship screening. We offered him a small grant, then brought him into a mentorship program. He devoured every book we gave him. Taught himself coding. Attended webinars from our partners in Dubai.

Last year, he got accepted into a premier engineering college with a full scholarship.

He sent us an email that said, "I will come back and build a school in my village."

I read that line at least ten times.

Because that is the multiplier effect of belief.

It starts with a book.

And ends with a building.

It starts with a chance.

And ends with a chain of changemakers.

That's why, even now, as our companies scale across verticals, from shipping to real estate to tech, I ensure that impact is not an afterthought. It is an operating principle.

Every deal we do, I ask: what lives does this touch?

Every project we launch, I ask: what values does this reinforce?

Because capitalism without consciousness is just conquest.

But with purpose, it becomes a community.

And that's what I'm building. Not an empire. A community of belief.

Where young people can dream not just of wealth, but of worth.

Where entrepreneurs can chase not just scale, but sincerity.

Where every success has a shadow of service.

And every structure we build, whether a villa, a ship, or a scholarship, carries the DNA of dignity.

That's why Karma Developers was never just about real estate.

It was about resonance.

About building spaces that felt aligned, balanced, and intentional.

And the same philosophy guides how I give back.

Not loud. But lasting.

Not performative. But personal.

Because giving is not an act. It's a posture.

You walk through the world differently when you know your rise can be someone else's root.

You speak differently when you've seen what silence can do to someone's spirit.

And you build differently when you understand that legacy is not what you leave behind, it's what you light within others.

As I close this chapter of my life's story, I carry a deep knowing: Success is not what I climbed. It's what I carried. It's who I chose to take along the way. It's the hands I held when they had nothing but hope. It's the voices I amplified when mine was the only one being heard. And above all, it's the knowledge that long after my name fades from headlines, these acts, quiet, consistent, sincere, will live on. In lives. In lessons. In legacies.

Because real giving is not about changing the world.

It's about changing the world.

One spark.

One soul.

One step at a time.

Sometimes, the most powerful act of giving is simply showing up when no one else does.

I remember being invited to speak at a small maritime institute in rural Maharashtra. No stage lighting. No media presence. Just fifty cadets in neatly ironed uniforms, sitting in plastic chairs, eyes filled with hope and hunger. They had read about me, yes. But they hadn't come for a celebrity entrepreneur. They had come for a glimpse of possibility.

I had planned to speak for twenty minutes.

I stayed for two hours.

Not because I had to.

Because I saw myself in them.

The wide-eyed questions. The quiet fears. The unspoken dreams of boys and girls who knew they weren't supposed to dream too big, but couldn't help it.

One of them asked, "Sir, what if you're the first in your family to ever do something like this?"

I smiled. "Then you build the staircase your children will climb."

That day, I didn't give them funding. Or a job. Or even internships.

What I gave them was permission.

To imagine.

To dare.

To begin.

And sometimes, that's all someone needs.

I've always believed that influence is not about how many people know your name.

It's about how many remember your impact.

Not in press clippings. But in personal shifts.

Not in applause. But in action.

A woman once approached me after a leadership summit in Dubai. She said nothing for the first few moments. Just stood there, slightly trembling, before finally saying, "You told a story about your grandfather once, about how you earned his trust, not demanded it. I started rebuilding with my own father after that."

She didn't need advice. Or acknowledgment.

She just needed to say it.

And I just needed to receive it.

Because giving back isn't only about what you give.

It's also about what you allow others to give you in return: trust, gratitude, transformation.

We often think of community as an external construct: villages, cities, teams, industries.

But the real community begins inside.

With the people you carry in your conscience. The stories you don't let go of. The values you refuse to compromise.

I've had moments where my own team members told me they felt seen for the first time in their careers, not because I raised their salaries, but because I remembered their child's name. Asked about their mother's surgery. Checked in when they were low, even if performance wasn't.

Those are moments of leadership. But more importantly, they're moments of giving.

Giving dignity.

Giving space.

Giving humanity back to workplaces that often forget what the word even means.

When I was younger, I used to equate success with scale.

Now, I equate it with significance.

How many lives did I elevate?

How many leaders did I shape?

How many silent battles did I make a little easier for someone else?

And in that sense, the scorecard looks very different.

There are names that will never appear in press articles or investor decks, but they are engraved in my journey.

A chartering assistant who went on to become a CEO.

A cleaner's son who now runs an ed-tech platform.

A junior officer who now owns a shipping line of his own.

I didn't just build companies.

I built conduits.

For hope. For mobility. For momentum.

And perhaps that is my true empire.

Not the assets or awards. But the access I created, for others.

Because here's the truth: power means little if it doesn't produce possibility.

We live in a world hungry for success, but starving for sincerity.

And if my path can offer even a fraction of that, I'll consider it sacred.

Recently, during an offsite with my core team, someone asked what the next five years looked like.

I paused.

Because for the first time, I didn't want to talk about new verticals, new investments, or even valuations.

I wanted to talk about the velocity of value.

I told them: "In five years, I want each of you to be mentoring others. Not just juniors. But outsiders. People who'll never work here. People who may never meet me. But who feel our presence in the way you lead. I want our influence to outpace our income. I want our ideas to infiltrate communities we've never even heard of. Because that is how you know you've built something bigger than yourself."

That's the vision now.

To build not just companies, but consciousness.

To create a legacy that breathes, teaches, multiplies, without me having to be in the room.

We're already planting seeds.

From community libraries in remote towns to skilling platforms for gig workers.

From funding minority-led startups to creating anonymous crisis helplines for professionals.

None of this is charity.

It is clarity.

The clarity that giving back is not a phase.

It's a framework.

A life architecture where everything you earn is looped back into something larger than you.

The Sanskrit word "seva" means service without expectation.

That's what I've grown into.

Not a philanthropist with a plaque.

But a practitioner of purposeful presence.

My wife, Mridula, reminds me of this constantly. Her quiet initiatives with women entrepreneurs, her way of empowering through elegance, her ability to uplift without spotlight, it all grounds me.

We often discuss this at home, not just what we're building, but what we're becoming.

Are we becoming more accessible?

More anchored?

More aligned?

Because that, too, is a form of giving: becoming the kind of person your younger self needed, and your future self can be proud of.

In closing this chapter, I don't want applause.

I want echoes.

Of voices I helped find.

Of journeys I helped unlock.

Of dreams that took flight because someone, somewhere, gave them the nudge they didn't even know they needed.

And if those echoes outlast me, I'll consider my work complete.

Because in the end, you are not remembered for what you had.

You're remembered for what you gave away freely.

And the way you made others believe in their own ascent.

Not by pointing them to a map.

But by being the living proof that it's possible to create a path, even when there's no map at all.

Chapter 9: The Unseen Struggles - Mental Health, Loneliness & Pressure

Success has many masks. I've worn most of them.

The boardroom mask that grins when the numbers work out, though your brain is repeating something bad that happened three hours ago.

The captain's mask that remains steadfast on the bridge of the ship during thirty-foot waves, though your stomach is in on the collapse.

The founder's mask that tells your team, "We're on the right track," though you're secretly wondering if the runway will hold.

But the actual face behind all those masks?

That's a face visible only to the mirror. And occasionally, even the mirror averts its gaze.

There's something nobody really prepares you for when you begin climbing: how the air at the top is different. It thins out, it quiets. The view could be incredible, but it is accompanied by a strange sort of quiet. Not peace, not liberty. Simply quiet. The kind that feels like a question that will get an answer.

I've spent decades building, from ships to startups, real estate to relationships. And yet, some of the hardest things I ever built weren't on spreadsheets or architectural blueprints. They were within me: resilience, self-belief, recovery. Especially recovery.

Not from failure, that's easy to talk about. But from emotional fatigue.

From burnout.

From the weight of being seen as unshakeable when, in fact, you're quietly breaking apart.

Let me take you back.

There had been a point, not long after Karma Developers had taken off in Dubai, when everything seemed picture-perfect.

Projects were pouring in.

The team was on board.

Public image was pure gold.

But within me, I was weary in a way I couldn't describe. It wasn't physical. I wasn't unwell. I was just fatigued. Soul-fatigued.

You see, after years of running, running first for survival, then growth, then influence, you lose how to stop. The mind doesn't recognize rest anymore. It begins to run in quiet, looking for a fire to extinguish or a mountain to climb. And when there's none, it becomes self-destructive. That's when it gets dangerous.

I started noticing things about myself. Little things at first.

I'd lie in bed late at night, performing calculations that didn't make a difference.

I'd become irrationally frustrated with small inefficiencies.

I stopped appreciating the things that used to make me feel full: walking, music, even lunch with Mridula. I was getting on, getting it done, even succeeding on the outside. But internally? I was silently going to pieces.

But I didn't mention it.

Because who do you tell it to?

Who do you call when you're the one they all call?

That is the dilemma. The more competent you look, the less room they leave for you to make mistakes. They think you have it all together. They assume strength from you even when you are trembling inside.

There was a morning, I recall well, when I remained in my car outside our Dubai office for more than an hour. I could not leave.

Not out of fear.

Not out of issue.

But simply because I did not have the energy to take a step in and deliver.

I was looking at the building, at the brand I had created, at the company I was passionately in love with, and I felt nothing.

It was then that I realized that something was wrong.

I went home that day. Told my assistant I had meetings elsewhere. Switched off my phone. Sat quietly for hours.

And then, I did something I hadn't done in years.

I wept.

Not with tears of sadness. But with tears of fatigue.

It was as if a dam was breached, and all those years of pressure, unspoken, unprocessed, burst forth.

The expectations.

The obligations.

The image.

The necessity to always be together.

It all fell apart in that moment of truth. And strangely, that downfall didn't kill me.

It freed me.

For the first time in a very long time, I ceased working and just let myself feel. That one action, permission to feel exhausted, not to be the better one, not to fix anything, was the start of my healing.

Not the sort that corporate newsletters or press releases write about. But the sort that saves your soul.

I did not attend a retreat. I did not schedule a therapy session, although I now highly recommend it. What I did was much more extreme for someone such as myself.

I slowed myself.

I began to rise early in the morning, but not to go to work. Instead, to sit in quiet.

I began reading again what had inspired me before, on a different note. These were not business books. Instead, I began reading philosophical books, poetry, and biographies of modest leaders.

I began walking with no direction. Me and the streets of Dubai before the city became alive.

I started writing once again. Not for others to read. Just for myself. To clear the noise within.

That minor activity, journaling, was my therapy.

Every page was a mirror. It made me aware of my fears, my anger, my guilt, and then my clarity.

I wrote everything: the urge to never stop developing, regrets about not being present during the important moments of my own children, feelings of isolation because I am always the one deciding, and the fear of even thinking that one question: what would I do in case I lose everything?

I never shared those pages with anyone. I still haven't. They're stored away, holy. Because in those words exists a me that was hurting. And healing.

What I came to understand in that time was this: leaders do break. We just don't speak about it.

We revere stoicism.

We praise hustle.

We celebrate 4 a.m. grind habits.

But we seldom ask: at what expense?

What I discovered in that slow drop and gradual ascent was that rest is not weakness. It's wisdom. It's rebellion in a world that celebrates endless motion. And once I experienced the clarity of stillness, I started creating systems around it.

You don't have to flee the world to be balanced; you must be deliberate in it. I made tiny, barely noticeable adjustments to my day-to-day rhythm, yet they cumulatively made a difference.

I broke my morning calls. My first hour of the day was no longer touched. No telephones. No inboxes. Only quiet, breath, and centering.

I would sometimes sit on my balcony sipping my coffee with my eyes closed, simply listening to the sounds of the city below. I would sometimes walk barefoot on the grass, reminding myself of the earth. It sounds silly, even decadent. But it kept me alive.

Because what's the value of empire-building if you lose yourself along the way?

There's one more thing I haven't mentioned yet, something that many founders, particularly in high-risk businesses like shipping and real estate, carry quietly.

Survivor's guilt.

Not in the classical sense, but in the entrepreneurial one. It's that nagging unease when you've succeeded, when the ships are afloat, the balance sheet is healthy, the press is clamoring for interviews, and yet, you think of those who began with you and did not.

The burnout co-founder.

The bankrupt friend.

The peer who remains mired, building, hustling, sleepless.

You start to feel like you don't deserve to slow down, to rest, to get tired. You think to yourself, "They're still in combat, and here I am, lagging behind?"

That is a corrosive guilt, just like burnout. Because it compels you to keep pushing upward, not because you're driven by ambition, but because you feel you need to.

I held that feeling for so long. Particularly after 2020, when everyone around me was fighting, companies were closing down, departments were laying off, and hopes were put on hold. And yet, somehow, Karma kept growing. We were recruiting. We were expanding.

Some days I felt like I couldn't broadcast our victories. As if they had to be concealed so someone else wouldn't feel the pang of comparison. I silenced aspects of my path to create room for theirs.

But now I realize: "Your light doesn't extinguish another's. If anything, it becomes a beacon that they can see from afar."

So I changed the topic, from "Here's what we accomplished" to "Here's what we learned." I quit just tweeting milestones and began tweeting mindsets. Because if I could make my own journey a roadmap to resilience, perhaps someone else would be able to sidestep the suffering I had to stumble through in the dark.

There's one specific night I'll never forget.

I had just exited a lengthy investor meeting. It had been good. We'd shut down a strategic round of funding that would position us for our next phase of growth. My team was partying. Mridula had cooked a special meal. And yet, as I entered my house, I felt a rush of nothing.

No happiness. No relief. Just a hollowness.

I slipped away quietly, made my way out to the balcony, and sat in darkness.

The city lights sparkled, the breeze was chill, and even so, I couldn't feel here. My head was a blank. Not serene blank, empty blank.

And in that instant, a question arose that I had put into dormancy for years: "Am I doing this for them, or for myself?"

You know, vision and validation walk a fine line between doing something because you think it's good and pushing because you must prove yourself. And I saw that I had stepped across that line more than once.

I was still in the lead. Still constructing. Still motivating. But a certain piece of me was doing it to fill a gap I had not yet defined. A desire to be validated, recognized, seen, maybe from childhood, maybe from failure, maybe just because we are all human.

And the bitter twist?

The more you validate people, the emptier it can be if it is not based on self-acceptance.

That night altered me. Not immediately. But it initiated a fresh level of self-work.

I started viewing my success as not identity, but as instruments.

I am not my business.

I am not my wealth.

I am not my media coverage.

I am the person who braved storms, rebuilt, took risks again, and still dared to look within.

That is my true success.

And as soon as I really did believe that, everything changed.

I started appearing more vulnerable in staff meetings. If I was exhausted, I let people know. If I was uncertain, I asked for feedback. If someone else could do it better, I took a backseat. My team did not lose their respect for me. They developed greater trust.

Because vulnerability is not a sign of weakness in leadership. It is what makes it authentic.

And gradually, I started establishing a rhythm with emotional sustainability.

Sleep was no longer optional. No "I'll sleep when I'm dead" for me. I ceased romanticizing burnout. I left social gatherings early. I avoided networking sessions that left me drained. I valued a smaller number of richer relationships over shallow friendships.

I went to therapy, not because I was in crisis mode, but because I craved clarity. I approached my mental health the same way I approached my legal advisors, my CFO, or my architects: with respect, regularity, and investment.

And I constructed what I refer to as my "circle of truth."

It's not big, four individuals. None of them work for me. None of them is concerned with my businesses. They are concerned with me. As an individual. As a man. As a dad. As a friend.

They are the ones whom I call upon when I need to shed the title and simply be.

Everybody needs that.

Leaders need it especially.

Because this journey isn't linear. It's not "win after win." It's messy. It's deeply human. And pretending otherwise is not strength, it's suffering in silence.

What I've learned, sometimes the hard way, is that nothing erodes inner peace faster than pretending you're okay when you're not.

As founders, leaders, or decision-makers, we've been conditioned to carry burdens silently. To always be "on." To wear masks, of composure, of competence, of certainty, even when our inner world is gasping for air. But I've seen too many brilliant people burn out not because they lacked capability, but because they lacked space.

Space to speak freely.

Space to fail safely.

Space to not know.

So I made that space for myself. And eventually, I opened it up to others.

At Aethon, I implemented closed-door check-ins, not only for business reviews but also for personal well-being. I was asking my leadership team questions they didn't see coming.

"Are you sleeping alright?"

"Do you feel heard?"

"What's stressing you beyond work?"

There was initial reluctance. And then, gradually, the truth began to come out.

One executive confessed that he was struggling with insomnia.

Another admitted she was on the verge of leaving, not for another job, but because she felt invisible.

We didn't lose her or him. Instead, both went on to become pillars of our next chapter.

All because someone asked the right question, not during an evaluation session, but in a human moment.

That's when it hit me: mental health isn't an aside in leadership. It's the ground that everything grows out of.

And just as you would never construct a tower on broken concrete, you can't construct an effective team on broken psyches.

This leads me to another deeply personal element: the pressure to be perceived as the "strong one" in your group.

It's a paradox.

When you walk with confidence and clarity, people think you never crack. They don't inquire about how you are. They don't check in. They think you must be fine. You become the anchor for others, but anchors also become heavy.

There were months where everyone leaned on me, family, friends, team, partners, yet I had no one to lean on.

Not because I lacked people. But because I had created a sense of self around being the one who fixes, who helps, who is present.

And to need help? That was like violating the role.

It took me years to learn to let go of that. Years to understand that strength is not about keeping it all.

It's about knowing when to pass it on, if only for a moment.

It's about having people you can send 2 a.m. messages to saying, "I can't today", and they don't ask why. They just appear.

One such time was during a big acquisition negotiation.

In theory, all the pieces fell into place. The cost, the timing, the plan. But something within me was not right. I couldn't sleep. I couldn't concentrate. My entire body was wired.

I phoned a friend, not a business owner, not a consultant, just someone who knew me outside of labels.

He replied: "You don't sound pumped. You sound drained."

And with that one sentence, I was returned to my essence.

I walked away from the deal. Everyone thought I was mad. Two months after we walked away, the company we had considered buying collapsed because of hidden liabilities. That one action of listening to my inner voice, amplified by someone who really knew me, saved us tens of millions.

That's the power of grounded relationships.

And yet, in an over-connected world, loneliness has never been higher. Notably for leaders.

It's ironic. We're with people, gadgets, information, but we're hungry for genuine connection. Not LinkedIn likes. Not conference compliments. But soul-deep connection. The kind where you don't have to justify your fatigue. You just breathe, and someone understands.

I've made it a point now to find those spaces for myself.

Sometimes it's a quiet dinner with someone who doesn't discuss business.

Sometimes, it's volunteering in a rural school away from the city's din.

Sometimes, it's sitting on the ocean, remembering who I was before the world reminded me who I had to be.

Because every leader, however evolved, needs reminders.

Of origin.

Of humanity.

Of why we began in the first place.

There's also another unspoken struggle most founders never talk about: the fear of irrelevance.

When you create something that works, people begin to expect you to be successful all the time. They await your next success. They're linking it to your previous success. And suddenly, you're no longer creating out of curiosity; you're creating to maintain perception.

I have seen this fear destroy empires. People cling to dying businesses. They don't reinvent. They simply overextend into things they don't know. Not out of vision, but addiction to validation.

But here's the truth: not every chapter needs to be larger than the last.

Sometimes the next step is smaller, but truer.

Sometimes, walking away is growth.

Sometimes growing quietly is a strength.

I needed to break my habit of dependence on momentum. To be comfortable with quiet. To know that even the moon has phases and doesn't push to shine every night.

And that brings me to maybe the most significant realization of this entire journey: Your mental health is not a luxury. It's a strategy for leadership.

When you're clear on the inside, your choices are cleaner.

When you're well-rested, your vision is clearer.

When you're grounded, your impact is longer-lasting.

And when you're full of emotion, you don't build from emptiness. You build from purpose.

So if you're reading this and you're exhausted, not the kind that sleep will cure, but soul exhaustion, I see you.

Breathe.

Pause.

Reclaim your power.

And remember:

You are not your last decision.

You are not your quarterly report.

You are not your pitch deck or your press release.

You are a human being, complicated, gorgeous, growing.

Lead like one.

One of the greatest ironies of modern leadership is that the very people driving transformation in the world often neglect the transformation within themselves. We keep building and scaling, creating and solving, but in the quiet hours, we sometimes forget how to just be.

I remember once being asked, after a major business exit, "So, what's next?"

I smiled graciously and gave the corporate reply, "We're exploring new verticals, considering strategic integration", but really, I had no idea.

I hadn't taken a breath, hadn't paused to consider, to process the experience. I was so intent on motion that I didn't allow myself to simply be present with the moment.

Looking back, I should have said: "Nothing is next. Now is enough."

That experience taught me that unless we specifically create space in our lives for presence, the world will drive us crazy with its constant call for performance.

Ambition is a lovely fire, but only if it is tempered with awareness.

I've watched entrepreneurs pursue scale so vehemently that they lose sight of why they began.

I've watched CEOs achieve all the milestones in their strategic plan and yet be unfulfilled.

And I've sat across billionaires who couldn't sleep at night without medication, because their minds were racing with worry, not tranquility.

So I began asking myself: What does success feel like, not look like, when no one is watching?

That one question changed everything.

Success started to feel like a quiet morning.

Like having an hour of undistracted attention with my daughter.

Like being able to turn down a lucrative offer if it did not feel right morally.

Like seeing a mentee become successful in an area where I have no expertise.

Like reading something non-business related without guilt.

And maybe more than anything, success started to feel like inner calm even when the outside world was frenetic.

That's what mental wellness did for me.

Not perfection. But presence.

Not control. But clarity.

Not constant hustle. But conscious hustle.

This experience also taught me to redefine legacy.

Legacy isn't the number of staff or the magnitude of your exit.

Legacy is the vibe you leave behind in spaces you no longer occupy.

It's the culture of leadership that remains after your departure.

It's the protégés who now mentor others.

It's the choice that you made a decade ago that continues to serve families now.

And it's the calm your team experiences, not only in working for you, but in your presence.

That type of legacy takes inner work. Not only operational greatness, but also emotional intelligence.

That's why today, I'm not coaching for performance alone, but for peace.

I don't only ask, "What are you building?" I ask, "What's building you?"

I don't simply talk about returns. I say, "What's coming back to your life as a result of your decisions?"

Because if you're growing your business but shrinking your soul, that is not scale. That is self-destruction.

So to all the leaders out there reading this, if you're leading a startup, a family business, a global business, or even simply leading your own life, here is what I want you to know:

You are permitted to slow down.

You are permitted to reset.

You are permitted to say, "I'm struggling."

And above all, you are permitted to pursue joy, not as a prize, but as a right.

The path will challenge you.

There will be times of uncertainty, exhaustion, betrayal, and collapse.

There will be days your own voice sounds far away and choices weigh heavily.

But you'll keep moving forward.

And one day, you'll turn around, not at the riches earned, but at the strength developed.

Not at the companies built, but at the character that's emerged.

Not at the deals closed, but at the lives changed.

Because in the end, leadership isn't a title we bear.

It's a truth we live.

And the greatest leaders?

They don't just dominate markets.

They master themselves.

That is the path I'm still on.

And if my story gives even one person the courage to seek help, to slow down, to reconnect with their breath, then every silent struggle was worth it.

Because in this age of noise, the greatest revolution is stillness.

And in this age of speed, the greatest luxury is peace.

So pause.

Breathe.

You’ve done enough.

You are enough.

And the world needs not just your ambition, but your wholeness.

Chapter 10: Legacy & Looking Forward

Legacy is a term folks like to toss around when they're finished constructing. As though it's a curtain call. A term you apply when applause dissipates.

But for me, legacy was never about conclusions.

It was about commencement, about what occurs when you've passed through the fire and passed the torch on.

You understand, I was never one of those men who was obsessed with how the world remembered him. I am the one who has always been more interested in what I am leaving in people I have influenced. Not in the headlines, not in the gestures, but in these little folds, in these little murmurings, still spreading, still extending in spite of the rock, long after that rock has been dropped below the waters.

Once, when there were neither cameras nor words, I sat alone in an empty office, late one night. The team had departed, the city had darkened, and the day had been won on paper. But what struck me wasn't pride. It was an odd quiet. The kind that only comes after years of action.

I remember the kid I once was, the one with a flimsy suitcase, a back of ideals, and no safety net in sight.

The one who couldn't miss but kept missing.

The one who trusted in instinct rather than instruction.

The one who had every fiber of his being believe that it would all eventually figure itself out.

And in some inexplicable way, it did.

But not the way the world anticipated.

Not because I constructed a business empire or headed multi-segment teams or braved financial milestones that once seemed dreamlike.

It made sense because I never lost sight of the reason I began.

The reason wasn't money. It was freedom.

The reason wasn't appreciation. It was alignment.

The reason wasn't size. It was significance.

I recall asking myself a question one day that would become a sort of compass throughout the years: If all of what I constructed was wiped away in one night, what would remain?

The response wasn't assets. It was an impact.

It was the cadet who got the promotion due to a letter of recommendation I had signed without fanfare.

It was the young entrepreneur whose first investor was my faith in them.

It was the tiny school we sponsored in a village that now boasts electricity and educators, and aspirations on walls.

That's legacy.

Not what you possess.

But what you pass on.

It took me decades to learn that the strongest moments of life don't appear like success at the time.

They appear like a sacrifice. Or silence. Or failure.

But they seed something. And if you're steady enough, and grounded enough, they grow in others years after you're gone.

There's a terrible beauty to leadership, particularly the type that's founded on vision rather than ego.

You bear heavy loads nobody notices.

You engage in battles nobody applauds.

And you make it a point to walk single so that others may walk en masse.

But if you do it correctly, if you start with integrity and finish with purpose, you don't just build companies.

You build people.

You build movements.

You build legacies that can't be erased when the lights go out.

I've had folks ask me, "What would you do differently if you could go back?"

And the truth?

Not much.

I would still take the harder path.

I would still bet on instinct.

I would still give away chances to others who were in greater need of them than myself.

Because each scar taught me a lesson.

Each detour defined the ultimate map.

And each loss honed the lens through which I view success today.

The world has a tendency to honor the finish line. But I've come to honor the footprints. The ones that remind me, I kept going, even when the landscape grew unforgiving.

There were times when I was trudging through fog. When the pressure of other people's and my own expectations weighed so heavily upon my chest that breathing itself seemed like a chore.

I've doubted my decisions. Pondered whether I was destined for simpler things. Considered vanishing altogether, just to find out if the world would even care.

But whenever I hit that edge, something drew me back.

Sometimes it was the sound of laughter from my daughter.

Sometimes it was a midnight text from a mentee.

Sometimes it was the still voice within me that whispered, Not yet. There's more to do.

And that is the thing about legacy, it doesn't wait until retirement.

It nudges you in the midst of your most hectic years.

It sits with you when nobody attends your launch.

It reminds you that even though the world may not be applauding, your work is important.

To someone.

Somewhere.

And that's all that matters.

Some of the most important things I've ever learned didn't happen from a mentor or a workshop. They occurred from being present with my own silence. You learn when you take away the noise, the judgment, the plans, the requirement to be more, do more, build more.

I recall a day, one of those seminal, intangible days that never make it into the media reels, where I cancelled appointments, silenced my phone, and drove for hours with no particular place to be.

I didn't require insight.

I needed to breathe.

I needed to be human again, not an affiliation, not a boardroom seer, but a man with questions greater than answers.

What occurred to me during that drive was not a business concept. It was not a strategy, not a breakthrough.

It was a very quiet, very honest epiphany: I had spent years constructing things that other people could see, but the things that others could not see mattered the most.

The trust I had earned.

The dignity I had fought for.

The values I had refused to budge on, even when it would have been more convenient, and more lucrative, to turn a blind eye.

That's the starting point on which I built it all.

And that's what I would like to be remembered for.

You see, when the lights go out, and they always do, it's the values that remain.

And those values have names.

Like fairness.

Like loyalty.

Like grit.

Like grace.

I don't think legacy is determined by what you initiate. Legacy is determined by what you maintain.

Anyone can have one stroke of good luck. Anyone can catch a wave.

But how many can create a tide of their own? How many can keep coming back, even when the thrill has worn off?

That's why I've never been fixated on exits.

I've cared more about the entrance. How individuals get into my life. How I get into theirs. If we exit each other in better shape than we entered one another.

A business transaction is simply a trade.

But trust?

That's the true currency.

And I've spent years, decades, guarding that currency as if it were gold.

Even in failure. Particularly in failure.

I've had enterprises that didn't fly. Markets that overnight turned against you. Promises broken by both sides. And every time, I could have slipped away quietly, attributing fault to circumstance.

But I remained. I called on every stakeholder. I owned up. I took losses personally, not as punishment, but as evidence that I still had skin in the game.

You can outsource operations.

You can outsource marketing.

But you can't outsource character.

That's the one thing only you get to control.

And if that's still standing, the rest is recoverable.

I've attempted to impart that, not merely in words of wisdom, but in example.

To my staff.

To my family.

To those young leaders who visit me looking for a way around it but depart with something greater: insight.

Because taking shortcuts is so appealing.

But it's nearly always costly.

What's unusual is constancy.

What's unusual is the principle.

What's unusual is a human being who doesn't chase noise, but builds signal.

If I could leave the next generation reading this a final piece of advice, it would be this:

Don't be remembered for your ascend.

Be remembered for your stretch.

How many did you raise?

How many did you shield?

How many will say, "Because of them, I didn't quit"?

That's legacy.

And here's the paradox: The more you invest in building others, the stronger your own foundation gets. That's not karma. That's physics. That's cause and effect.

Along the way, I learned to stop asking, How much more can I do? and began to ask, How much more can I mean?

That changed everything.

It made me invest differently.

Hire differently.

Speak differently.

Live differently.

And yes, even dream differently.

Because a dream, when it turns solely into you, becomes too small.

Real dreams are permeable.

They spill over into others.

They create possibilities beyond your own requirements.

They sow seeds in people you'll never know.

And that's when your life starts to resonate.

Long after you're gone.

One night, not so long ago, I sat across a young founder in one of Dubai's quieter backstreets in a coffee shop nestled in one of its lesser-known corners. He had that certain fire burning in his eyes, that same flame that I used to carry with me into shipping terminals, into interview chairs, onto foreign shores with a dream stored in my pocket.

He asked me something I wasn't prepared for. Not "How did you succeed?" or "What's the next big thing?"

He wanted to know, "How did you remain kind?"

That question struck me more than any spreadsheet or balance sheet has ever been able to.

Because the reality is, kindness is the hardest part of this path.

The world does not always pay back kindness.

Business is cruel.

People let you down.

Systems are unjust.

But if you let that make you hard, if you begin to play the game the rest of the world does just in order to survive, you win in the world's eyes, and you lose in your own.

So I said to him: I didn't remain kind because it was easy. I remained kind because I couldn't afford to lose the one thing about myself that made all this worthwhile.

Empathy.

Fairness.

Patience.

Being willing to listen when it's inopportune.

To know when it's better to understand than to judge.

That is what makes you strong. That's what has people following you, not because they're afraid, but because they respect you.

Because sooner or later, all the records you pursued will be broken by someone else.

But character? That is the one competitive edge that cannot be duplicated.

I've had deals fall through because I refused to play dirty.

I've walked away from lucrative opportunities because they came with ethical compromises.

And you know what? I've never regretted it.

Not once.

Because peace of mind is a kind of wealth most people forget to chase.

And I chased that with the same intensity I chased every deal, every opportunity.

Even today, when I am mentoring young entrepreneurs, I don't only discuss valuation and pitch decks. I ask them: "How are you sleeping at night?"

Because if your mind is not peaceful, your vision will fade.

If your soul is rambunctious, your strategy will tank, regardless of how well-funded it is.

At night, when no eyes are watching, you will know this: every choice, every sacrifice, every act of bravery, you hold it with you. It becomes your reflection. And I've worked to keep my mirror clean. Not flawless. Just true. Because I have done wrong. Misjudged people. Overjudged allies. Underjudged danger. But I have always worked to make

The mercy shown when I could have exacted revenge.

The silence I opted for instead of vindication.

Those are the moments I hold dearest.

Because legacy isn't boisterous.

It's constructed in whispers.

In integrity.

In the way you treated people when they had nothing to give back to you.

And if there is one thing I want you to learn from all this, it is this:

You don't have to be great to the world.

You just have to be consistently true in the eyes of your own soul.

When I started off on this journey, from ships to boardrooms, from grit to grace, I believed legacy was about leaving something behind that you've built.

Now, I know better.

Legacy is about how you built it.

It's about the stories people will tell about you long after you've left the room. Not the press clippings, not the LinkedIn accolades, but the dinner table conversations. The quiet admiration. The respect that lingers when your name comes up.

And that only happens when you live aligned, with your purpose, your principles, and your people.

In this next phase of my life, I'm no longer building just for returns.

I'm building for resonance.

Karma Developers is no longer just a company. It's a consciousness. A way of seeing the world through the lens of long-term value, not short-term wins.

Aethon, my first love, remains my test of discipline and discretion.

Silkleaf, the family office, is my method of educating future generations not only in how to create wealth, but in how to cultivate wisdom.

And the Karma Foundation? That is my soul at work. My childhood aspirations manifested as real hope for others. It's where my legacy takes a breath, in education, empowerment, and compassion.

What do people wonder about the next 10 years?

And I have plans, naturally, I do, but I also have peace.

I no longer need to prove myself.

I only need to keep appearing, with presence, not pressure.

To remain curious.

To remain useful.

To remain true.

That's the only KPI that matters to me now.

And to those still climbing: I see you.

I salute your hustle.

But I want you to stop, just for a moment, and consider asking yourself this: Am I creating something that means something? Or merely something that is impressive?

Because someday, when the lights are low and the clapping has stopped, that's the only thing that will remain.

What mattered. Who you raised up. And how you made your life add up to more than mere milestones.

And as I put this book down, not as an ending, but as a stepping forward, I share with you this one honest truth:

You already have all you need.

It's not in the money.

It's not in the connections.

It's not even in the plan.

It's in the fire you burn.

The belief you hold dear.

The silence you respect.

The action you take, day after day, with no crowd, no payoff, just raw intention.

That is the start of your legacy.

And it's already happening.

So walk on.

With grace.

With courage.

With clarity.

And when you arrive at your idea of "the top," keep in mind: someone, somewhere along the way, stood on your shoulders to reach. Do the same for someone else.

Because true leaders don't merely build.

They elevate.

They include.

They light up.

And in so doing, they leave behind something more than success.

They leave behind significance.

That's what I have done too, throughout my journey, and even now.

What truly brings me joy isn't just business milestones or market wins, it's watching the people around me succeed.

I find myself, almost unknowingly, guiding others to invest wisely, nudging them to consider entrepreneurship, or encouraging a young student to pause and reflect on what truly excites them. It could be a casual conversation with a driver, a chat with a barber, or a moment with someone from my grandfather's village. These aren't just encounters, they're reminders of the potential we all carry, often waiting to be noticed.

Entrepreneurs have always been my tribe, not just CEOs, but the self-made, the street-smart, the bold souls who turn courage into livelihood. And when I see them thrive, it stirs something deeper in me than any personal success ever could.

I am also surrounded by the kind of wealth no ledger can measure: loving parents, supportive siblings, nephews who look up to me, in-laws who stand by me, a partner who believes in me, children who teach me patience, and friends who know me beyond titles.

This is my abundance.

And perhaps that's why chasing more money or fame doesn't define me anymore. I've already been given so much.

Legacy, to me, isn't about what I build for the world; it's about what I awaken in people.

So now, as the final page turns, I leave you not with a roadmap, but with a mirror.

This was never a manual. It was a memory of grit, of growth, of grace under fire.

If anything I've lived or shared has sparked even a flicker within you, then let that be your beginning. Because my legacy isn't in these words, it's in what you do after reading them.

Build your life like it matters.

Love like it heals.

Lead like it lasts.

And when your own story is written, let it not be remembered for how high you climbed, but for how deeply you lived.

This is where my telling ends. But perhaps, it's where your becoming begins.

Verses Kindler Publication

Verses Kindler Publication

Reach us through our website

https://www.verseskindlerpublication.com/

For more information visit our Instagram or Facebook page.